301110

your
health

EXPRESS NEWSPAPERS

non-retirement guides

your health

How to keep fit, prevent illness and manage your health care

Edited by Frances Kay

KOGAN
PAGE

Publisher's note

Every possible effort has been made to ensure that the information contained in this book is accurate at the time of going to press, and the publishers and the author cannot accept responsibility for any errors or omissions, however caused. No responsibility for loss or damage occasioned to any person acting, or refraining from action, as a result of the material in this publication can be accepted by the editor, the publisher or the author.

First published in Great Britain in 2009 by Kogan Page Limited

Kogan Page Limited
120 Pentonville Road
London N1 9JN
United Kingdom
www.koganpage.com

© Kogan Page, 2009

The right of Kogan Page to be identified as the author of this work has been asserted by them in accordance with the Copyright, Designs and Patents Act 1988.

British Library Cataloguing in Publication Data

A CIP record for this book is available from the British Library.

ISBN 978 0 7494 5585 9

Typeset by Jean Cussons Typesetting, Diss, Norfolk
Printed and bound in Great Britain by MPG Books Ltd, Bodmin, Cornwall

Contents

Introduction   1

1 Lifestyle   3
   General Advice   3
   Yoga   6
   Sensible eating   6
   Food safety   9
   Drink   10
   Smoking   12

2 Prevention and care   15
   Accident prevention   15
   Aches, pains and other abnormalities   16
   Health insurance   17
   Private patients without insurance cover   21
   Long-term care insurance   23

Permanent health insurance   27
Health screening   27
Hospital care cash plans   29
National Health Service   30
Benefits   33
Prescriptions   34
Going into hospital   35
Alternative medicine   39
Eyes   41
Feet   46
Hearing   47
Teeth   48
Personal relationships   51
Depression   54
Some common afflictions   56
Some special problems   63

3 **Disability**   **69**
Transport   74
Powers of attorney   75
Temporary living-in help   77
Permanent living-in help   80
Flexible care arrangements   81
Emergency care for pets   84
Practical help for carers   85
Holiday breaks for carers   87
Benefits and allowances   89
Financial assistance   94

Summary   **97**

Introduction

Retirement should be a time for positive good health. Many people have spent years indoors working in offices or suffering a daily journey to work. Keeping fit and healthy while holding down a demanding job requires a lot of self-discipline as well as excellent time management. Now that you have retired, you will have more chance to be out in the fresh air or take up a sport again. You won't have to rush your meals and, without the need for business lunches or sandwiches day after day, you could easily knock off a few pounds without much effort at dieting. At the same time, there will be less temptation to drop into the pub on the way home, or collapse into a chair with a glass of wine in your hand at the start of the evening.

Most people admit that one of the major gains of retirement is not having to fight their way to work in the rush hour;

those interminable journeys on buses and trains, jam-packed with people in various states and conditions. The winters are always worst, with people next to you coughing and sneezing; or sitting in stuffy carriages with no fresh air. What about the delays, on public transport and in traffic, which had the effect of raising your blood pressure. Once free of the strains and pressures that are part of any job, you will feel less harassed and look better. If you are cutting down on fattening snacks too, you will find you have the energy to devote to new interests and activities.

People can get aches and pains of course as they become older. Doctors will tell you, again and again, this is far less likely if you remain physically and mentally active. In other words, the days for putting on slippers and regarding retirement as the onset of old age are definitely gone. Today's recently retireds are often younger in age, looks and behaviour than any previous generation. They can therefore look forward to many healthy years ahead.

As with anything else, however, bodies do require a modicum of care and attention if they are to function at their best. Just as your car needs regular servicing, routine checks such as eye testing and dental appointments are obviously sensible. Also, moderation, middle-aged as it may sound, is generally a wiser policy than excess. This has nothing to do with treating yourself as a premature geriatric – quite the reverse. It means enjoying small vices without paying the penalty for over-indulgence. By keeping trim (instead of getting out of shape) and making the effort to look good and keep alert, you are likely to have a far longer and more enjoyable retirement.

1

Lifestyle

General advice

Of paramount importance is to remain fit and healthy. Good health is the most valuable possession we have. Without it, energy is lacking, activities are restricted and the fun goes out of life. No amount of money can compensate for being bed-ridden or a semi-invalid. Although anyone can be unfortunate enough to be struck down by an unexpected illness, your future good health is largely in your own hands. The reason why people in their 70s are so often dogged by aches and pains is that insufficient care has been taken by them during their 50s and 60s. As well as all the obvious advice about not smoking, becoming overweight or drinking to excess, there is the important question of exercise. Although doing press-ups or going for walks will help, there are many more interesting ways of keeping fit.

Exercise plays an important part in keeping you healthy whatever age you are. It tones up muscles and improves the circulation. It reduces flab, helps ward off illnesses such as heart disease and, above all, can be a great deal of fun. The experts' motto is: little and often. For those not accustomed to regular exercise, it is essential to build up gradually. If you are planning to run a marathon or win the local tennis competition, start gently. If you rush off to play squash with your son or grandson, or recapture the sporting feats of your youth, you may get carted off to hospital or the doctor's surgery while still wearing your tracksuit.

Training in a whole range of sports is available around the country, with beginners in their 50s and older especially welcomed. In addition to some of the more exotic choices, swimming has long been recognised as one of the best forms of exercise. Some people say there is nothing to beat a good brisk walk. Gardening is also recommended. With the explosion of sports clubs, leisure centres and adult keep-fit classes run by local authorities and other organisations, opportunities have never been better for athletes of all ability levels – or none.

At the top end of the market, there are de luxe health clubs located in hotels, sports clubs and other commercial operators. These offer, among other things, facilities such as a fitness centre, swimming pool, massage and beauty salon. They have qualified staff who can advise on – and supervise – personal fitness programmes. However, at a fraction of the price, many local authority leisure centres offer a marvellous range of sports. They also usually run regular classes in everything from self-defence to badminton.

Emphasis and availability in every type of keep-fit activity is on the increase. It is a welcome innovation as there are a growing number of opportunities for older people and those with disabilities. If you cannot find the information locally, search the internet. Otherwise, the following organisations may be able to help you.

Extend, now celebrating its thirtieth year, aims to enhance the quality of life for over-60s and disabled people of all ages by providing structured recreational movement sessions to music. For information about classes in your area, contact: Tel: 01582 832760; e-mail: admin@extend.org.uk; website: www.extend.org.uk.

The Fitness League is a national organisation whose aim is to promote fitness in an atmosphere of 'happy informality'. Emphasis is on exercise and movement to music, with special regard to individual ability. There are classes suitable for all ages, with some participants in their 70s. For further details, contact: Tel: 01344 874787; e-mail: tfl@thefit-nessleague.com.

Medau Movement was developed in Germany at the beginning of the 20th century. Recreational movement classes aim to provide enjoyable lessons that improve posture and muscle tone, while developing suppleness, strength and stamina. There are also special breathing exercises, influenced by yoga, which are designed to aid respiration and stimulate the circulation. Classes are held all over the country. For further information, contact: Tel: 01403 266 000; email: office@medau.org.uk; website: www.medau.org.uk.

Yoga

The number of yoga enthusiasts is increasing year by year and it is estimated that over half a million people in Britain regularly practise yoga as a means of improving fitness and helping relaxation. Classes are provided by a great many local authorities; there are also a number of specialist organisations. Below, are two that arrange courses in many parts of the country.

British Wheel of Yoga is the governing body for yoga in Great Britain. It has over 2,000 teachers around the country and runs classes suitable for all levels of ability. Fees vary according to class size and area of the country. Some classes have special rates for retired people. For further information, contact: Tel: 01529 306851; e-mail: office@bwy.org.uk; website: www.bwy.org.uk.

Iyengar Yoga Institute runs classes at all levels, including remedial for those with medical conditions. Of special interest is the 59-plus class for people who would like to start gently. For further details, contact: Tel: 0207 624 3080; e-mail: office@iyi.org.uk; website: www.iyi.org.uk.

Sensible eating

A trim, well-kept body is one of the secrets of a youthful appearance. Excess weight and being out-of-condition tends to adds years to anyone's age. Regular exercise is one-half of the equation, sensible eating the other. It is reported that over one in four adults in Britain is obese – that is, seriously overweight. No one is going to worry about the odd two or three pounds, but half a stone or more not only begins to look unsightly but starts to become a health risk. Middle-aged men in particular run the increased risk of a heart attack. But carrying excess weight can lead to other illnesses and makes operations more difficult. The older one gets, the greater the likelihood of restricted mobility.

Before embarking on a serious diet, it is important first to consult your doctor. But medical advice does not need to be sought if you are thinking of cutting out or cutting down on sweets, cakes, sticky buns, deep-fried foods, alcohol and rich sauces. Healthy foods that most people (except of course those on a doctor's special diet) can eat in almost unlimited quantities are fruit, salad, vegetables, fish and white meat such as chicken.

You should also keep an eye on your cholesterol level. Excess cholesterol (fatty deposits that collect in the arteries) is a great concern because although it is regarded as a problem affecting the overweight, slimmer people can also suffer from it. The basic health message is eat low-fat, healthy food; include plenty of roughage such as wholemeal bread in the diet. It is important to cut down on dishes with a high sugar, salt and animal fat content – this particularly includes cream, butter and red meat.

As every health magazine advises, crash diets are no solution for long-term fitness. This is because unless individuals re-educate their eating habits, the weight comes back within a few days or weeks. Many people need a boost to get started and one increasingly popular method is sponsored dieting for charity. Another possibility, which some people swear by and others rubbish, is going to a health spa. As opposed to starvation, the emphasis today is on a few days' general fitness eating (but usually enough to avoid being hungry). If nothing else, the experience is very relaxing, though not cheap, with average costs being in the region of £175 to £250 a day. There are many advertisements for such places in the national press, at the back of glossy magazines. Your friends would probably be happy to recommend their favourite places, or search the internet.

Cheaper and arguably more successful for long-term slimmers are Weight Watchers' meetings, held across the United Kingdom. The aim of Weight Watchers is to help members establish a healthy, balanced approach to weight loss, with emphasis on making small, lifetime changes that can be maintained for the long term. There are two different food plans: a 'Points' plan, where all food is given a points' value, allowing members flexibility in their food choices; and a 'No Count' plan, where members can eat three meals a day from a prescribed list of foods from each food group. For details, contact: **WeightWatchers** Customer Service: Tel: 0845 345 1500; email: uk.help@weightwatchers.co.uk; website: www. weightwatchers.co.uk.

Of particular interest to women is the Natural Health Advisory Service, formerly known as the Women's Nutritional Advisory Service. This organisation maintains that many of the problems associated with the menopause can be alleviated without recourse to hormone replacement therapy (HRT) by healthy eating and exercise. For further information, contact: **Natural Health Advisory Service:** Tel: 01273 609699; email: enquiries@naturalhealthas.com; website: www.naturalhealthas.com.

If you are single, you may find that living on your own presents a number of issues regarding food. Some people tend to get weight problems, perhaps because they cannot be bothered to cook for themselves, so snack off the wrong kinds of food such as jam sandwiches and chocolate biscuits. Alternatively, they neglect themselves and do not take enough nourishment. Elderly women, in particular, sometimes quite literally hardly eat enough to keep alive. In consequence, not only do they undermine their health but because of their general frailty they are more susceptible to falls and broken bones. Two excellent gifts for anyone living alone or for couples whose family has flown the nest are: *Easy Cooking for One or Two* by Louise Davies, Penguin, £6.99, and *Leith's Cooking for One or Two* by Polly Tyrer, Bloomsbury, £12.99. Self-help to avoid trouble is one thing, but anyone who suspects that they could have something wrong with them should not hesitate to consult their doctor.

Food safety

No discussion about food and eating would be complete without a word or two on the subject of food safety. As most readers will know, it is inadvisable for anyone to eat raw eggs, whether consumed steak-tartare fashion or used in uncooked dishes such as mayonnaise and mousses. To be on the safe side, elderly people as well as the very young should probably also avoid lightly cooked eggs. Likewise, if, as was the case several summers ago, there is an official warning about certain seafood, then it is only common sense to refrain from eating the items in question.

However, when it comes to food poisoning, eggs and seafood are far from being the only culprits. It's been widely reported in the press that people tend to shop only once a week for perishable food, so the risks are high of eating items that are no longer as fresh as they should be. 'Cook-chill' foods in particular, including ready-cooked chickens and pork pies, are a breeding ground for bacteria, especially in the summer when many foods – even vegetables – are liable to deteriorate more quickly. Storage and cooking also play a major part in warding off the dangers of food poisoning. The government leaflet *Preventing Food Poisoning* gives the following basic advice:

▨ keep all parts of your kitchen clean;

▨ aim to keep your refrigerator temperature at a maximum of 5° C;

▨ keep raw and cooked foods separate and use within the recommended dates;

▨ cook foods thoroughly;

▨ do not reheat food more than once and don't keep cooked food longer than two days.

Drink

Most doctors cheerfully maintain that 'a little bit of what you fancy does you good'. The majority of healthy adults can enjoy a drink at a party or a glass of wine with dinner without any ill effects and retirement is no reason for giving up these pleasures. In small quantities alcohol can be a very effective nightcap and can also help to stimulate a sluggish appetite. However, where problems begin is when people fancy more than is good for them. Alcoholism is the third greatest killer after heart disease and cancer.

The condition is far more likely among those who are bored or depressed and who, perhaps almost without realising it, drift into the habit of having a drink to cheer themselves up or to pass the time when they have nothing else to do. The trouble is that the habit can become insidious. At the beginning it does not feel that way, so individuals can quite quickly start becoming dependent on drink. Because the early symptoms appear fairly innocuous, the danger signs are apt to be ignored. These can include: needing a drink as a confidence boost; having 'just one more' out of misplaced conviviality at the end of a party; drinking in the morning to cure a hangover; drinking on your own; keeping a spare bottle 'just in case'; and having sneak drinks when you think no one is noticing.

Whereas most people are sensible enough to be able to control the habit themselves, others may need help. The family doctor will of course be the first person to check with for medical advice. But additionally, for those who need moral support, the following self-help groups may be the answer.

Alcoholics Anonymous has over 3,000 autonomous groups all over the country, designed to help those with a serious alcohol problem learn how to stay sober. Through friendship and mutual support, sufferers assist each other in coping, which is made easier by meeting others with the same problem. Meetings take two forms: some are for members only; others are open to relatives and friends. Membership is free, although a voluntary collection is taken towards the cost of renting meeting rooms. For more information, contact: Tel: 0845 769 7555; email: help@alco-holics-anonymous.org.uk; website: www.alcoholics-anony mous.org.uk.

Al-Anon Family Groups UK & Eire offer support and understanding where a relative's or friend's drinking is causing concern. Of possible interest to worried grandparents, Alateen, a part of Al-Anon, is specifically for teenagers aged 12–20 whose lives are or have been affected as a result of someone else's drinking. There are over 850 groups throughout the UK and Ireland. Contact: Tel: 020 7403 0888; email: enquiries@al-anonuk.org.uk; website: www.al anonuk.org.uk.

Alcohol Concern is a charity, a national umbrella body for 500 local agencies, tackling alcohol-related problems. It aims to promote better understanding and improve services for those in need of help. It publishes a quarterly magazine, has a library and a small bookshop and can supply addresses of local advice and information centres. Contact: Tel: 020 7264 0510; email: contact@alcoholconcern.org.uk; website: www.alcoholconcern.org.uk.

Smoking

Any age is a good one to cut back on smoking or preferably to give up altogether. The gruesome facts are that smokers are 20 times more likely to contract lung cancer; they are at more serious risk of suffering from heart disease, particularly coronary thrombosis; and additionally are more liable to chronic bronchitis as well as various other ailments.

Most people agree that it is easier to give up completely than attempt to cut back. Every habitual smoker knows that after the first cigarette of the day you can always think of a thousand excuses for lighting another. Aids to willpower include the recent ban on smoking in restaurants, bars and pubs and other designated areas, and leaving your cigarettes behind when you go out. Also helpful is not buying cigarettes for guests to smoke in your home, which they leave but you take. Finally, the best tip is refusing as a personal point of honour to cadge off friends. Many hardened smokers also swear by nicotine patches, available from most chemists. Working out how much money you could save in a year and promising yourself a holiday or other reward on the proceeds could help. Thinking about your health in years to come should be an even more convincing argument.

Dozens of organisations concerned with health publish leaflets giving the facts, including the harm you can do to non-smokers. To list just a couple that provide information:

Quitline offers information, advice and counselling for smokers and ex-smokers alike. Contact: Tel: 0800 00 22 00; email: stopsmoking@quit.org.uk; website: www.quit.org.uk.

Smokeline (Scotland only) offers free advice, counselling and encouragement to those wishing to give up smoking. Available noon to midnight, seven days a week. Contact: Tel: 0800 84 84 84.

There is now also an **NHS Smoking Helpline,** which offers help and advice to smokers who want to quit, and it can give information about local cessation services, including nicotine replacement therapy, one-to-one counselling and group support. The service also welcomes calls from ex-smokers who have given up but need a little support to help them not return to smoking. Contact: Tel: 0800 022 4 332; website: www.nhs.uk/gosmokefree.

2

Prevention and care

Accident prevention

One of the most common causes of mishap is an accident in the home. In particular this is due to falling and incidents involving faulty electrical wiring. The vast majority of these could be avoided by taking normal common-sense precautions. This could be something as simple as repairing or replacing worn carpets and installing better lighting near staircases.

If you are unlucky enough to be injured in an accident, whether in the street or elsewhere, the Law Society offers a free service called The Accident Line to help you decide whether you can make a claim. You will be entitled to a free consultation with a local solicitor specialising in personal injury claims. He/she will inform you whether you have a good case, how to go about claiming and how much you might claim. Should you decide to pursue the matter, you are under no obligation to ask the same solicitor to act for you. A similar service is offered by The National Accident Helpline; for further details, contact: **The Accident Line:** Tel: 0800 19 29 39; website: www.accidentlinedirect.co.uk, **National Accident Helpline:** Tel: 0800 376 0185; website: www.national-accident-helpline.co.uk.

Aches, pains and other abnormalities

There is nothing about becoming 50, 60 or even 70 that makes aches and pains an inevitability. Age in itself has nothing to do with the vast majority of ailments. However, a big problem is that many people ignore the warning signs when something is wrong, on the basis that this symptom or that is only to be expected as one becomes older. More often than not, treatment when a condition is still in its infancy can either cure it altogether or at least help to delay its advance. The following should always be investigated by a doctor, to allay fear or to get treatment at an early stage:

▦ any pain that lasts more than a few days;

▦ lumps, however small;

▦ dizziness or fainting;

▦ chest pains, shortness of breath or palpitations;

▓ persistent cough or hoarseness;

▓ unusual bleeding from anywhere;

▓ unnatural tiredness or headaches;

▓ frequent indigestion;

▓ unexplained weight loss.

Health insurance

An increasing number of people are covered by private health insurance or provident schemes during their working lives. If you wish to continue this benefit, and you are unable to remain in your company scheme after retirement, you will normally be welcomed as an individual client by most of the main groups provided you are under the age of 70 (or, in some cases, even older). You can then renew your membership when you do reach 70. Even if you have not previously been insured, it is not too late to consider doing so. Although obviously this would be an extra expense, should you be unfortunate enough to fall ill or need an operation and want to be treated as a private patient, insurance would save you a great deal of worry and expense.

The terms and conditions of the different schemes offered by health insurance groups vary to some extent. All the major ones offer to pay, if not all, at least the greatest part of the costs. These include inpatient accommodation, treatment and medical fees, as well as outpatient charges for specialists, X-rays and similar services. They do not normally cover GPs' costs. Subscription levels largely depend on the area in which you live and on the type of hospital to which you choose to be admitted. The top figure is usually based on charges in private hospitals in London; the next is based on private hospitals outside London; and the lowest rate is based on charges in NHS paybeds and some private hospitals.

Other factors that can substantially affect the price are: your age; the extent of the cover offered; and the various restrictions – or exclusions – that may apply. Many insurers have recently introduced a range of budget policies that, although they have the advantage of being less costly, are naturally also less comprehensive. For example, some policies confine cover to surgery or only cover certain specified procedures. Particular illnesses, or conditions, may be excluded, as may outpatient treatment. There may be an annual cash limit or the policy may include an excess – that is, the subscriber pays a fixed amount of every claim, typically between £100 and £500. Another popular saving are policies that restrict private care to cases where the wait for NHS treatment would exceed 6 (sometimes 12) weeks. As with all types of insurance, the small print matters, so look carefully at all the plans available before selecting the scheme that best suits your needs.

The NHS has, generally, an excellent record in dealing with urgent conditions and accidents. However, it sometimes has a lengthy waiting list for the less urgent and more routine operations such as hip replacements and hernias. By using health insurance to pay for private medical care you will probably get faster treatment, as well as greater comfort and privacy in hospital. The major organisations that provide cover are described below:

BUPA is the largest of the provident associations and offers a variety of choices for individuals under its Heartbeat plan. Customers are given a personalised price, according to which benefits they specifically choose to have included in their policy. It is possible to limit cover, for example, just to cancer and heart conditions. Alternatively, you can opt for a more comprehensive policy covering a wider range of eventualities, including cover for most existing health problems. Guidance and support are available 24 hours a day from a team of nurses. Subscriptions can be reduced by electing to take an annual excess option, paid once, not for every claim you make in the year. For further information, contact BUPA: Tel: 0800 600 500; website: www.bupa.co.uk.

AXA PPP offers a range of medical insurance policies to cover the cost of private health care. All include access to the Health at Hand counselling and health information line – a confidential 24-hour service staffed by nurses, pharmacists and counsellors with whom customers can discuss any health issues that concern them. Benefits and monthly subscriptions vary according to an individual's health, lifestyle and geographical area. Customers who pay by single annual premium receive a 5 per cent discount. For further information, contact AXA PPP: Tel: 0800 121 345; website: www.axappphealthcare.co.uk.

Exeter Friendly Society is a non-profit-making friendly society with subscribers throughout the United Kingdom and overseas. Its private health insurance has three distinguishing features that may make it particularly attractive to people of retirement age: it accepts new subscribers of any age up to 80; premiums are not increased on account of age, so rates for older people may be lower than many other schemes; making a claim will not result in an increase in your next premium. For further information, contact: Tel: 08080 55 65 75; website: www.exeterfriendly.co.uk.

Other groups that offer health insurance plans relevant to people over retirement age include:

BCWA Healthcare. Tel: 0800 197 6997; website: www.bcwa.co.uk.

Legal & General Healthcare. Tel: 0800 096 6959; website: www.legalandgeneral.com.

Norwich Union Healthcare Ltd. Tel: 0800 056 7654; website: www.norwichunion.com.

Saga Services Ltd. Tel: 0800 857 857; website: www.saga. co.uk.

Help with choosing a scheme

With so many plans on the market, selecting the one that best suits your needs can be quite a problem. If you would welcome advice, you can either ask an independent financial adviser for help or approach a specialist insurance broker, such as those listed below.

Mercer Limited operates an advice service to help you choose a health care plan most likely to suit your personal circumstances. Contact: Tel: 0117 988 7533; website: www. mercer.com.

Medibroker offers advice on the best available health care plans. Contact: 0800 980 1082; email: ukclientservices@ medibroker.com; website: www.medibroker.co.uk.

The Private Health Partnership will provide genuine, independent and unbiased advice on searching for a cost-effective health scheme to match your specific needs. Contact: Tel: 0124 588 862; email: info@php.co.uk; website: www. php.co.uk.

Private patients without insurance cover

If you do not have private medical insurance but want to go into hospital in the United Kingdom as a private patient, there is nothing to stop you. That is to say, provided your doctor is willing and you are able to pay the bills. More and more people are forgoing insurance in favour of paying for themselves, if and when the need arises. The choice if you opt for self-pay lies between the private wings of NHS hospitals, hospitals run by charitable or non-profit-making organisations (such as the Nuffield Hospitals) and those run for profit by private companies. To help meet the cost, a number of health insurance providers have launched a variety of purpose-designed plans that normally consist of a regular savings account, plus optional insurance to provide cover towards part of the bill. Also helpful, if you cannot pay the full cost immediately is to arrange an interest-free loan (for repayment within 10 months) for treatment at certain hospitals. One provider of such a service is: **Nuffield Hospitals**: Tel: 0800 688 699; website: www.nuffieldhospitals.org.uk.

An interesting alternative

Have you ever thought of combining a holiday and having an operation at the same time? Sounds curious, but you could investigate one of the latest growth areas in health care – Health Tourism. Health and Medical Tourism is where you travel to take advantage of less-expensive health treatments. These include cosmetic, dental, spa treatments, medical procedures (including joint replacement, heart surgery and other elective procedures). You can save usually over 50 per cent on the fees that you would pay for private treatment in United Kingdom – and have a holiday as well. The destinations are extensive and sometimes exotic. Leading health tourism destinations include Eastern Europe, the Baltic Region, Malta, Cyprus, Turkey, the Middle East, India, Malaysia, Singapore, South Korea, Costa Rica and Argentina. One way to find out about this new and growing market and to meet some of the providers of such services is to visit the Health Tourism Show held annually at Olympia, in London. For further information on this subject, contact: **The Health Tourism Show**: Tel: 01372 743837; website: www.healthtourismshow.com; or **Treatment Abroad**: Tel: 01442 817817; website: www.treatmentabroad.com.

Long-term care insurance (LTCI)

An emergency operation is one thing; long-term care because an individual can no longer cope unaided, quite another. Over the past few years, a number of insurance companies have launched policies designed to help meet the costs in the event of a person needing to stay long term in a nursing home or requiring a carer to look after them in his/ her own home. The days when the welfare state automatically picked up the bill no longer exist. Anyone with total assets of more than £13,000 will be expected to contribute according to their means, while those with capital of over £21,500 including the value of their home will not qualify for assistance and will need to support themselves from their savings. (**NB:** A married couple would not be forced into selling their home if the other partner were still living there.)

Average nursing home fees now cost around £35,000 a year. Care in your own home, if you were ever to become seriously incapacitated, is likely to be at least as expensive. It is advisable, if you can, to make some provision against long-term care. The big advantages of insurance cover of this type are that it buys peace of mind and would help safeguard your savings should care ever become a necessity in the future. An additional plus point is that benefits paid out to a policyholder are tax-free.

However, although a godsend in case of need, none of the policies is exactly cheap and in most cases the criteria for paying out are pretty stringent. Cover normally only applies if an illness is diagnosed after joining and although some plans cover a wide range of eventualities, others specifically exclude some of the critical illnesses such as cancer. The premiums, which can be paid on a regular annual basis or as a lump sum, vary considerably, as of course does the amount of financial assistance given. In all cases, the charges are largely determined by the subscriber's age at time of first joining and, as you would expect, are very much cheaper at 55 than 75.

To avoid wrangles over eligibility for benefit, most of the schemes have adopted a system, known as activities of daily living (ADLs). ADLs typically include: bathing/washing, dressing, feeding, going to the lavatory, and getting in and out of a bed/chair. The higher the number of these an individual is unable to manage on their own, the greater their benefit entitlement. In some policies, Alzheimer's disease is specifically covered.

Although pre-funded insurance is the cheapest way of buying care cover, a disadvantage is that if you never claim you lose all the money you have paid over the years. Some policies link the insurance with an investment, providing a payout on death if no claim has been made. Though initially more expensive, you can take your money out of the plan at any time. However, if the investment growth is poor you could lose some of your capital. Companies offering long-term care policies include **Norwich Union Healthcare Ltd**: Tel: 0800 056 7654; website: www.norwichunion.com; and **Partnership Assurance**: Tel: 0845 108 7240; website: www. partnership.co.uk.

A possible alternative to a conventional long-term care policy is **critical illness insurance**, which pays a lump sum if you are unfortunate enough to be struck by one of a specified number of dread diseases, such as cancer or a stroke. Rather than pay into a policy ahead of time, an alternative solution that has been growing in popularity is to buy a **care fee annuity** (sometimes known as an immediate-needs annuity) as and when the need arises. Such annuities can be bought with a lump sum and, as with other annuities, pay an income for life. The income is normally considerably higher than normal annuity rates but with no return of capital to benefit your successors (capital protection is available with higher contributions). An advantage, however, is that you would only buy a care plan at such time as it would actually be useful. A further plus point is that all money paid by the policyholder direct to the care provider, including a home nursing agency, is free of tax.

Despite these attractions, care fee annuities are not all win–win. First, you would be investing a sizeable chunk of capital, which, depending on your life expectancy, may or may not prove good value in the long term. Also, as recent research by the Care Funding Bureau shows, prices quoted by different companies to provide exactly the same annual income often differ by many thousands of pounds and although there may sometimes be a good reason for this, if you are interested in the idea you would be well recommended to obtain several quotes. Companies offering care fee annuities include: Norwich Union, AXA PPP Lifetime Care and Partnership Assurance. Contact: **Norwich Union Healthcare Ltd**: Tel: 0800 056 7654; website: www.norwichunion.com; **AXA PPP**: Tel: 0800 121 345; website: www.axapphealthcare.co.uk; **Partnership Assurance**: Tel: 0845 108 7240; website: www.partnership.co.uk.

Deciding on your best option is not easy, since quite apart from the cost, all such policies are restrictive in one way or another. You are strongly advised to shop around and to read the small print extremely carefully before signing. If, as may be suggested, you are thinking of investing some of your lump sum to pay for the policy, it would be sensible to ask a lawyer or financial adviser to check the documentation for any hidden drawbacks. Alternatively, and this might be the best idea, you could ask an independent financial adviser (IFA) to recommend what would be your best choice. Two organisations worth contacting for advice on finding an IFA or on long-term care are: **IFA Promotion Ltd**: Tel: 0800 083 0196; email: contact@ifap.org.uk; website: www.unbiased. co.uk; and **NHFA Ltd**: Tel: 0800 99 88 33; email: enquiries@nhfa.co.uk; website: www.nhfa.co.uk.

However good the advice, only you can decide whether some form of long-term care cover would be a sensible precaution. As with most major items of expenditure, there would inevitably be arguments for and against. However, whereas in the past the market was something of a jungle, you may be reassured to know that, since October 2004, all LTCI products and services must now come under the compulsory jurisdiction of the Financial Ombudsman Service and the Financial Services Compensation Scheme. In accordance with the new rules, not only must the sales literature provide clear information about the key features of the policy, including whether premiums are subject to review, but all advisers are required to pass an appropriate exam to ensure that they have the relevant competence to help customers make an informed choice about the type of product and amount of cover they need. The **FSA** also has a helpful factsheet, *Choosing a Financial Adviser – How key* *facts can help you*; available from the FSA on Tel: 0845 606 1234; website: www.fsa.gov.uk.

Permanent health insurance (PHI)

PHI should not be confused with other types of health insurance. It is a replacement-of-earnings policy for people who are still in work and who, because of illness, are unable to continue with their normal occupation for a prolonged period and in consequence suffer loss of earnings. Although highly recommended for the self-employed, many employees have some protection under an employer's policy. Either way, if you are close to retirement, PHI would be unlikely to feature on your priority list.

Health screening

Prevention is better than cure and most of the provident associations offer a diagnostic screening service to check general health and to provide advice on diet, drinking and smoking if these are problem areas. These tests show that roughly a quarter of patients aged over 55 have an unsuspected problem that can often be treated quickly and easily. Screening services normally recommend a check-up every two years and centres are usually available to members of insurance schemes and others alike.

BUPA. There is a network of BUPA Wellness Centres up and down the country, offering a range of health assessments. In most cases, same-day results can be provided so that you can discuss the findings with your health adviser and doctor there and then. Prices vary but tend to be less expensive for men. For further details, contact BUPA on Tel: 0800 616 029; website: www.bupa.co.uk/wellness.

BMI Healthcare offers a range of screens at its hospitals. Screens, known as Personal Health Profiles, cost slightly more for women than men. For further information, contact BMI Healthcare on Tel: 0808 101 0337; website: www. bmihealthcare.co.uk. E-mail: info@bmihealthcare.co.uk.

National Health Service. The NHS offers several different screening services of particular relevance to those aged 50-plus. Two are especially for women and the others are more general. First, all adults who have not been seen by a GP over the last three years can request an appointment for an assessment of their general health. This will include a few simple tests, such as checking your blood pressure, and the opportunity to discuss any health problems that could be worrying you, as well as discussion of factors to do with your lifestyle that could be affecting your health. All patients over 75 should be offered an annual health check by their GP, which could be arranged in their own home if they prefer. As well as their general state of health, the check will cover such matters as eyesight, hearing, possible mobility problems, worries that might be causing depression, use of medicines and similar.

The special tests for women are to screen for breast cancer and abnormalities of the cervix. These tests are available in all parts of the country. All women aged between 25 and 64 who are registered with a GP are offered a smear test every three to five years, depending on their age. Women aged between 25 and 49 receive invitations every three years. Those aged between 50 and 64 receive invitations every five years. Tests are also available to women aged 65-plus who have not been screened since age 50 or who have had a recent abnormal test.

All women aged between 50 and 70 years are invited for screening by breast X-ray every three years. Although women aged over 70 no longer receive routine invitations, if they have any reason for concern, they should speak to their GP to arrange an appointment. If for some reason you have not been receiving invitations for screening, you should ask your GP for details or enquire at your local primary care trust. For further information, see leaflets *NHS Cervical Screening – the facts* and *NHS Breast Screening – the facts*, both obtainable from GPs and primary care trusts. For further details on NHS services, see website: www.nhs.uk.

Hospital care cash plans

These schemes provide a cash sum for every night the insured person spends in hospital. Premiums can start from just £1 a week, giving a payment of about £18 a night. All benefits are tax-free and are available to anyone joining before age 65. A number of schemes cater for individuals aged over 65. About 20 organisations offer such schemes as well as a wide range of other health insurance, including cover for optical and dental treatment. A list can be obtained from: **British Health Care Association (BHCA Service Ltd):** Tel: 0153 651 9960; website: www.bhca.org.uk.

National Health Service

Most readers will need no introduction to the National Health Service. However, there are one or two scraps of information that you may not know – or possibly have forgotten – that may come in useful around retirement. One area is the range of professionals, including district nurses and occupational therapists, who can provide invaluable support if you are caring for an elderly relative or if a member of the household requires to go into hospital.

Choosing a GP

If you move to a new area, you will need to find a new doctor. The best way to choose one is normally by recommendation. If you do not know who to ask you can write to, or call in to, your local primary care trust or strategic health authority. Alternatively, you can search the NHS website: www.nhs.uk.

You could ask to consult the local medical directory, where you will find details of GPs' qualifications and special areas of knowledge. This could be useful if someone in the household has a particular health problem and you would feel happier with a doctor who has more specialised experience.

Additional points you may want to consider are: how close the doctor is to your home; whether there is an appointments system; whether it is a group practice and, if so, how this is organised. All GPs must have a practice leaflet, available at their premises, with details about their service. The information should include: names, addresses, sex, year of qualification and type of qualifications, along with essential practice information such as surgery hours, services provided and arrangements for emergencies and night calls.

Having selected a doctor, you should take your medical card to the receptionist in order to have your name registered. This is not automatic as, first, there is a limit to the number of patients any one doctor can accept. Also, some doctors prefer to meet potential patients before accepting them on their list. If you do not have a medical card, you will need to fill in a simple form.

If you want to change your GP, you go about it in exactly the same way. If you know of a doctor whose list you would like to be on, you can simply turn up at his/her surgery and ask to be registered; or you can ask your local primary care trust, or health board in Scotland, to give you a copy of their directory before making a choice. You do not need to give a reason for wanting to change and you do not need to ask anyone's permission.

Two useful publications to read are *You and Your GP During the Day* and *You and Your GP at Night and Weekends*, available free from libraries, strategic health authorities and doctors' surgeries.

NHS Direct

If you need medical advice when you are on holiday or at some other time when it may not be possible to contact your doctor, you could ring **NHS Direct**, which offers a 24-hour free health advice service, staffed by trained nurses. The

number to call is Tel: 0845 46 47; website: www.nhsdirect.
nhs.uk.

Help with NHS costs

If you or your partner is in receipt of income support,
income-based job seeker's allowance or the pension credit
guarantee credit, you are both entitled to free NHS prescriptions, NHS dental treatment, NHS wigs and fabric supports,
and an NHS sight test. You are both equally entitled to the
maximum value of an optical voucher to help towards cost
of glasses or contact lenses and payment of travel costs to
and from hospital for NHS treatment. You are also entitled
to help if you and/or your partner are entitled to, or named
on, a current tax credit NHS exemption certificate.

Even if you are not automatically entitled to help with the
above costs, you and your partner may be entitled to some
help on the grounds of low income. To find out, fill in claim
form HC1 – obtainable from social security or Jobcentre
Plus offices as well as many NHS hospitals, dentists, opticians and GPs – and send it to the Health Benefits Division
in the prepaid envelope provided with the form. If you are
eligible for help, you will be sent a certificate that is valid
for up to 12 months according to your circumstances.
Depending on your income, you may receive an HC2 certificate, which entitles you to full help with NHS costs, or alternatively an HC3 certificate, which will entitle you to partial
help.

For more details see leaflet HC11 *Help with Health Costs*,
available from Post Offices, some pharmacies and GP surg-

eries, or contact the **Department of Health Publications** Orderline on Tel: 0870 155 5455; website: www.dh.gov.uk.

Benefits

If you are on income support and have a disability, you may be entitled to certain premiums on top of your ordinary income support allowance. There are four rates: £25.25 (single), £36.00 (couple) for the generally disabled, £48.45 for the severely disabled, and £96.90 if both partners qualify as severely disabled. Various social security benefits are also available to those with special problems because of illness. These include:

▪ Attendance Allowance, see leaflet DS 702;

▪ Disability Living Allowance, see leaflet DS 704;

▪ Employment and Support Allowance, see website www.dwp.gov.uk/esa.

Employment and Support Allowance

Incapacity Benefit was replaced by Employment and Support Allowance (ESA) from October 2008. ESA is a new integrated contributory and income-related allowance. The government has brought forward 'Permitted Work' rules in incapacity benefit into both elements of the new Employment and Support Allowance benefit. All ESA claimants can work for fewer than 16 hours and earn up to £86 per week for up to 52 weeks without losing their entitlement. For further information, including the special concessions for voluntary and permitted work, see website www.dwp. gov.uk/esa.

Prescriptions

Both men and women aged 60 and over are entitled to free NHS prescriptions. Additionally, certain other groups are entitled to free prescriptions. These include those on low income (see 'Help with NHS costs', page 34) and people who suffer from a specified medical condition. If you are not sure if you qualify, you should pay and ask the pharmacist for an NHS receipt form FP57, which tells you how to claim a refund. For further information, see leaflet HC11 *Help with Health Costs*, obtainable from Post Offices, some pharmacies and GP surgeries.

People who do not qualify but who require a lot of prescriptions could save money by purchasing a prescription pre-payment certificate. This costs £27.85 for three months, or £102.50 for a year. A pre-payment certificate will work out cheaper if you are likely to need more than five prescription items in three months, or more than 14 items in 12 months, as there is no further charge regardless of how many prescription items you require. If you prefer, rather than pay for the 12-month certificate in one go, you can make 10 monthly direct debit payments. Application form FP95 is obtainable from pharmacies and GP surgeries, or contact NHS Help With Healthcare Costs on Tel: 0845 850 0030; website: www.ppa.org.uk.

Going into hospital

Stories abound of people who wait months and months for an operation because of a shortage of beds. But although waiting lists for a hernia or hip replacement may be depressingly long in one area, hospitals in another part of the country may have spare capacity. Many patients are unaware that they can ask their GP to refer them to a consultant at a different NHS trust or even, in certain cases, help make arrangements for them to be treated overseas. Before you can become a patient at another hospital, your GP will of course need to agree to your being referred. A major consideration will be whether the treatment would be as clinically effective as you would receive locally.

Waiting lists have reduced considerably over the past few years, thanks to the government's initiatives in this area. This is of little comfort, however, if you are currently on a waiting list for treatment and feel that your condition has deteriorated and become more urgent. In this case you should speak to your GP, who may be able to arrange with the hospital for your appointment to be brought forward. See also 'Complaints', below.

Those likely to need help on leaving hospital should speak to the hospital social worker, who will help make any necessary arrangements. Help is sometimes available to assist patients with their travel costs to and from hospital. If you receive income support, income-based jobseeker's allowance or pension credit guarantee credit, you can ask for repayment of 'necessary travel costs'. If you are not sure what would qualify, you can check with the hospital before you travel. If you have a war or MOD disablement pension, you may get help with travel costs for treatment of your pensionable disability. There are special schemes for people who live in the Isles of Scilly or the former Scottish Highlands and Islands Development Board area. Claims for help can also be made on the grounds of low income. For detailed information, see leaflet HC11 *Help with Health Costs*. Call NHS Help With Healthcare Costs on Tel: 0845 850 0030; website: www.ppa.org.uk.

If you go into hospital, you will continue to receive your pension as normal. This was not always the case. Your pension – as well as incapacity benefit, severe disablement allowance, income support and pension credit guarantee credit – will continue to be paid in full, without any reductions, for the duration of your stay. For further information, see leaflet GL12 *Going Into Hospital?* obtainable from social security or Jobcentre Plus offices and NHS hospitals; see websites: www.jobcentreplus.gov.uk or www.dwp.gov.uk.

If you have any complaints while in hospital, you should speak to someone close to the cause of the complaint or to the complaints manager within the hospital; if the matter is more serious, you should write to the chief executive of the hospital. See also information below.

Complaints

The NHS has a complaints procedure if you are unhappy about the treatment you have received. In the first instance, you should speak to someone close to the cause of the problem, such as the doctor, nurse, receptionist or practice manager. If, for whatever reason, you would prefer to speak to someone who was not involved in your care, you can speak to the complaints manager at your local NHS trust or strategic health authority instead; addresses will be in the telephone directory. In jargon terms, this first stage is known as **local resolution**.

If you are not satisfied with the reply you receive, you can ask the NHS trust or strategic health authority for an **independent review**. The complaints manager will be able to tell you who to contact about arranging this. If you are still dissatisfied after the independent review, then the Health Service Ombudsman (known formerly as the Health Service Commissioner) might be able to help. The Ombudsman is independent of both government and the NHS. He/she investigates complaints of failure or maladministration across the whole range of services provided by, or for, the NHS, including pharmacists, opticians and dentists, as well as private hospitals and nursing homes if these are paid for by the NHS. The Ombudsman cannot, however, take up legal causes on a patient's behalf. Addresses to write to are:

Health Service Ombudsman for England: Tel: 0845 015 4033; email: phso.enquiries@ombudsman.org.uk; website www.ombudsman.org.uk.

Health Service Ombudsman for Wales: Tel: 01656 641 150; e-mail: ask@ombudsman-wales.org.uk; website: www.ombudsman-wales.org.uk.

Scottish Public Services Ombudsman: Tel: 0800 377 7330; email: ask@spso.org.uk; website: www.spso.org.uk.

If you have a complaint, you should get on to the matter fairly speedily or your complaint may be dismissed on grounds of being 'out of time'. Time limits require you to register complaints within 12 months of the incident or within 12 months of your realising that you have reason for complaint. These time limits may be waived if you have a very good reason why you could not complain sooner.

If you need further advice on the complaints procedure, contact **POhWER ICAS,** an independent complaints advisory service, on Tel: 0845 337 3065; website: www.pohwer. net.

Rather than proceed through the formal channels described above, an alternative approach – which of course does not prevent you from also applying to the Ombudsman or to anyone else – is to contact The Patients Association. This is an independent advice centre that offers guidance to patients in the event of a problem with the health service. The Association also publishes a selection of useful leaflets and a quarterly magazine – *Patient Voice.* The Patients Association, contact: Tel: 0845 608 4455; e-mail: helpline@ patients-association.com; website: www.patients-association.com.

Useful reading

Your Guide to the NHS, obtainable from the **Department of Health Publications** Orderline on: Tel: 0870 155 5455; website: www.dh.gov.uk.

Alternative medicine

Alternative medicine remains a very controversial subject. Some doctors dismiss it out of hand. Many patients claim that it is of great benefit. We list here some of the better-known organisations.

British Acupuncture Council (BAcC). Treatment, using fine needles, is claimed to be effective for a wide range of illnesses, including arthritis, rheumatism, high blood pressure and depression. The BAcC can provide you with a list of professionally qualified acupuncture practitioners in your local area. Contact: Tel: 020 8735 0400; e-mail: info@acupuncture.org.uk; website: www.acupuncture.org.uk.

British Chiropractic Association. Practitioners specialise in mechanical disorders of the spine and joints and the effects on the nervous system. Treatment is mainly by specific manipulation without drugs or surgery. For a list of members in your area, contact: Tel: 0118 950 5950; e-mail: enquiries@chiropractic-uk.co.uk; website: www.chiropractic-uk.co.uk.

British Homeopathic Association. Homeopathy is essentially natural healing that follows the principle of looking at the whole person rather than just the illness. Homeopathy is available on the NHS but as yet not many doctors are trained in this branch of medicine. The Association can supply a list of practising GPs as well as the names and addresses of pharmacies that stock homeopathic medicines. Patients wanting NHS treatment can only apply to GPs in their catchment area or get a letter of referral to one of the

homeopathic hospitals or to a GP able to take NHS refer-
rals. Otherwise, patients can be treated anywhere by doctors
on a private basis. Contact: 0870 444 3950; website: www.
trusthomeopathy.org.

British Hypnotherapy Association. Hypnotherapy may help
people with phobias, emotional problems, anxiety, migraine,
psoriasis or relationship difficulties. For details of the
nearest registered trained hypnotherapist, including his/her
qualifications and fees, plus a pamphlet answering common
questions about hypnotherapy, contact: Tel: 020 8579 5533;
website: www. hypnotherapy-association.org. When contacting the Association it would be helpful to indicate the
nature of your problem.

Incorporated Society of Registered Naturopaths. Naturopaths are concerned with the underlying conditions that may
cause illness, including, for example, diet, general fitness,
posture, stress and the patient's mental outlook on life. The
Society can put you in touch with your nearest practitioner.
Contact: Tel: 0131 664 3435; email: info@naturecure
society.org; website: www.naturecuresociety.org.

National Institute of Medical Herbalists. The practice of
herbal medicine aims to offer the sufferer not just relief from
symptoms but an improved standard of general health and
vitality. For further information and a register of practitioners, contact: Tel: 01392 426022; email: info@nimh.
org.uk; website: www.nimh.org.uk.

Osteopathic Information Service. Osteopathic treatment is
often appropriate for those with back problems or with
muscle or joint disorders. It can also provide pain relief from

arthritis. Advice and leaflets are available on request; or you can telephone for a list of osteopaths in your area. Contact: Tel: 020 7357 6655; email: info@osteopathy.org.uk; website: www.osteopathy.org.uk.

Wessex Healthy Living Centre. The Centre is a non-profit-making registered charity that, as well as having an educative purpose, runs a clinic where all natural therapies are available under one roof. Annual membership of the Centre is £20, or £25 for families. Members enjoy the benefit of reduced clinic fees and also receive a bi-annual newsletter and information leaflets. Contact: Tel: 01202 422087; email: info@wessexhealthylivingcentre.org; website: www.wessexhealthylivingcentre.org.

Eyes

It is advisable to have your sight checked at least every two years. Sight tests are now free on the NHS for all men, as well as women, aged 60 and over. If you are not yet 60, you can only get a free NHS sight test if: you are registered blind or partially sighted; are prescribed complex lenses; are diagnosed as having diabetes or glaucoma; if you are over 40 and are a close relative of someone with glaucoma (ie, parent, brother, sister, son or daughter); or if you are a patient of the hospital eye service or have been referred by them to an optometrist. You are also entitled to a free sight test if you or your partner is getting income support, income-based jobseeker's allowance or pension credit guarantee credit. You may also be entitled to some help if you are entitled to, or named on, a valid NHS Tax Credit Exemption

Certificate. For details, see leaflet HC11 Help with Health Costs: website: www.direct.gov.uk.

Even if you do not belong to any of these groups but are on a low income, you may be entitled to a free, or reduced cost, sight test. To find out if you qualify for help, you should fill out claim form HC1, which you can get from social security or Jobcentre Plus offices: websites: www.dwp.gov.uk; www.jobcentreplus.gov.uk.

People with mobility problems who are unable to get to an optician can ask for a domiciliary visit to have their eyes examined at home. This is free for those with an HC2 certificate or who are in receipt of one of the benefits listed above. People with a (partial help) HC3 certificate can use this towards the cost of a private home visit by their optician. The going rate for private sight tests if you do have to pay is about £20. Many opticians, however, charge less for people who are retired or run special promotions at various times of the year. Even if this is not advertised in the window, you have nothing to lose by asking before booking an appointment.

As you probably know, you do not need a doctor's referral to have your eyes tested. Simply book an appointment with a registered optometrist or ophthalmic medical practitioner. If you qualify for help with the cost, remember to take your HC2 or HC3 certificate, or other written evidence, with you to show to the optician. The sight test should establish whether or not spectacles are required and should also include an eye examination to check for signs of injury, disease or abnormality. Whether you have to pay or not, the optician must either give you a prescription identifying what type of glasses you require or alternatively give you a statement confirming that you have no need of spectacles. The prescription is valid for two years. If you do not use it straight away, you should keep it safe so that it is handy when you need to use it. When you do decide to buy spectacles or contact lenses, you are under no obligation to obtain them from the optician who tested your eyes but can buy them where you like.

There is a voucher system for helping with the purchase of glasses or contact lenses. If you or your partner are in receipt of income support, income-based jobseeker's allowance or pension credit guarantee credit, you will receive an optical voucher, with a cash value (April 2008/09) of between £35.50 and £196.00 (more for bifocals). The amount you get will depend on your optical prescription. If you do not get any of the above benefits but are on a low income, you may still be entitled to help. To find out fill in claim form HC1, as explained above: websites: www.adviceguide. org.uk; www.dwp.gov.uk.

The voucher might be sufficient to pay for your contact lenses or spectacles outright, or it may only make a small contribution towards the cost. Part of the equation will depend on the frames you choose. You will not be tied to any particular glasses: you can choose specs that cost more than the value of the voucher and pay the difference yourself. For further details, see leaflets HC11 *Help with Health Costs* (available in large print size) and HC12 *NHS Charges and Optical Voucher Values*. People who are registered blind are entitled to a special tax allowance (2008/09) of £1,800 a year.

A great deal of practical help can be obtained by contacting the Royal National Institute of Blind People. In addition to giving general advice and information, it can supply a range of special equipment, details of which are listed in a free catalogue. There are also a number of leaflets relating to blindness. For information, contact the **Royal National Institute of Blind People (RNIB)**: Tel: 0845 766 9999; email: help@rnib.org.uk; website: www.rnib.org.uk.

Many elderly people with failing sight suffer from macular degeneration that affects their ability to distinguish detail. Although there is no known cure individuals can be helped to make the most effective use of their sight by special magnifiers and other aids, such as clip-on lenses that fit over normal spectacles. For further information, contact: **Partially Sighted Society**: Tel: 0844 477 4966; website: www.patient.co.uk.

Another helpful organisation is the National Library for the Blind and The Talking Book Service, which lends books and music scores in Braille and Moon free of charge, and post-free, to any blind reader who registers with the service. It also offers a wide range of electronic library and reference services through its website. For information, contact: **National Library for the Blind and Talking Book Service**: Tel: 0845 762 6843; e-mail: cservices@rnib.org.uk; website: www.rnib.org.uk.

Blind, visually impaired and print-disabled people can enjoy national newspapers and magazines on audio tape, audio CD, digital and electronic formats. Contact these two organisations: **Talking Newspaper Association of the United Kingdom (TNAUK)**: Tel: 01435 866102; e-mail: info@

tnauk.org.uk; website: www.tnauk.org.uk; and **Talking News Federation (TNF)**: Tel: 0871 226 5506; e-mail: enquiries@tnf.org.uk; website: www.tnf.org.uk.

Yet another useful resource for those with limited vision is the special range of radio/radio cassette equipment provided by **British Wireless for the Blind Fund (BWBF)**. Equipment is provided free of charge to those in need, or sold through BWBF Direct. For further information, contact: **BWBF**: Tel: 01634 832501; e-mail: info@blind.org.uk; website: www. blind.org.uk.

For gardening enthusiasts, there is *Come Gardening*, a quarterly magazine available on audiotape and in Braille, and the **Cassette Library for Blind Gardeners**, which is offered as an auxiliary service to subscribers. There are also residential courses for blind gardeners. For further information, contact: **Thrive**: Tel: 0118 988 5688; website: www.thrive. org.uk.

Also worth knowing, all the main banks will provide statements in Braille; and Barclaycard now also issues credit card statements in Braille, on request. Additionally, several institutions offer large-print cheque books or templates for cheque books as well as other facilities, such as a taped version of their annual report. There is no extra charge for these services.

Finally, BT has a free directory-enquiry service for customers who cannot read or handle a phone book. To use the service you first need to register with BT, which will issue you with a personal identification number. Full details and an application form can be obtained from the registration department by calling Freefone 195; website: www.bt.com.

Feet

Many people forget about their feet until they begin to give trouble. Corns and bunions if neglected can become extremely painful; ideally everyone, especially women who wear high heels, should have podiatry treatment from early middle age or even younger. One of the problems of which podiatrists complain is that because many women wear uncomfortable shoes they become used to having painful feet and do not notice when something is more seriously wrong. The result can sometimes be ingrowing toenails or infections. Podiatry is available on the National Health Service without referral from a doctor being necessary, but facilities tend to be very over-subscribed, so in many areas it is only the very elderly or those with a real problem who can get appointments. Private registered chiropodists are listed in the *Yellow Pages*: website: www.yell.com.

Alternatively, you can write to The Society of Chiropodists and Podiatrists, which is the professional association for registered chiropodists and podiatrists, asking for some local names from their list. In addition to keeping a list of members, the Society can supply a number of free leaflets on foot health; contact **The Society of Chiropodists and Podiatrists:** Tel: 020 7234 8620; website: www.feetforlife.org.

Help the Aged has produced a helpful leaflet called *Fitter Feet*, which advises on how to avoid problems, gives tips on buying shoes and provides information on where to go for further help and treatment. Available from Help the Aged: Tel: 020 7278 1114; email: info@helptheaged.org.uk; website: www.helptheaged.org.uk.

Hearing

As they grow older, a great many people suffer some deterioration in their sense of hearing. Should you begin to have difficulty in hearing people speak, or find that you have to turn up the television, it is probably worth having a word with your doctor. Your GP may well refer you to a consultant who will advise whether a hearing aid would be helpful, or alternatively may refer you direct to a hearing aid centre for examination and fitting. You can either obtain a hearing aid and batteries free on the NHS or you can buy them privately.

There are many other aids on the market that can make life easier. BT, for example, has a variety of special equipment for when a standard phone becomes too difficult to use. For further information, dial BT free on: Tel: 0800 800 150 and ask for a free copy of *Communications Solutions*; website: www.bt.com.

There are also a number of specialist organisations that can give you a lot of help, both as regards hearing aids and on other matters.

Hearing Concern LINK – the newly united charity – provides support and information to people with hearing loss, as well as their families. For further information please visit the website: www.hearingconcernlink.org; e-mail: info@hearingconcernlink.org; Tel: 01323 638230

RNID publishes a comprehensive range of free leaflets and factsheets for deaf and hard-of-hearing people. Titles include: *The Facts – Hearing aids*; *The Facts – Losing your* *hearing*; and *The Facts – Equipment*. Contact: Tel: 0808 808 0123; email: informationline@rnid.org.uk; website: www. rnid.org.uk.

British Tinnitus Association (BTA). Tinnitus is a condition that produces a sensation of noise, for example hissing or ringing, in the ears or head. The BTA helps to form self-help groups and provides information through its quarterly journal, *Quiet*. Contact: Tel: 0800 018 0527; e-mail: info@tinnitus.org.uk; website: www.tinnitus.org.uk.

British Deaf Association (BDA) works to protect the interests of deaf people and also provides an advice service through its regional offices. Contact: Tel: 02476 550936; e-mail: midlands@bda.org.uk; website: www.bda.org.uk.

Friends and family can do a great deal to help those who are deaf or hard of hearing. One of the essentials is not to shout but to speak slowly and distinctly. You should always face the person, so they can see your lips, and avoid speaking with your hand over your mouth or when smoking. It could also be helpful if you, as well of course as deaf people themselves, were to learn British Sign Language. In case of real difficulty, you can always write down your message.

Teeth

Everyone knows the importance of having regular dental check-ups. Many adults, however, slip out of the habit, which could result in their having more trouble with their teeth as they become older. Dentistry is one of the treatments for which you have to pay under the NHS, unless you have a low income. Charges are based on 80 per cent of the cost up to a current maximum (April 2008/09) of £194. If you or your partner is in receipt of income support, income-based jobseeker's allowance or pension credit, you are entitled to free NHS dental treatment. You may also receive some help if you are in receipt of the working tax credit; for details, see leaflet HC11 *Help with Health Costs*, obtainable from Post Offices, some pharmacies and GP surgeries.

Even if you do not belong to any of these groups, you may still get some help if you have a low income. To find out if you qualify fill in claim form HC1 (obtainable from social security or Jobcentre Plus offices, NHS hospitals and NHS dentists). To avoid any nasty surprises when the bill comes along, it is important to confirm with your dentist before he treats you whether you are being treated under the NHS. This also applies to the hygienist should you need to see one. Best advice is to ask in advance what the cost of your treatment is likely to be.

Help with the cost is all very well but, for many, an even bigger problem than money is the difficulty of finding an NHS dentist in their area. Best advice is to call the British Dental Health Foundation's helpline, see below; or, if you are thinking of going private, ask friends and acquaintances for recommendations. You could also look in the *Yellow Pages* (website: www.yell.com) where you should find some names.

Denplan. For those who like to be able to budget ahead for any dental bills, Denplan could be of interest. It offers two plans: Denplan Care, which for a fixed monthly fee (average £20) entitles you to all routine and restorative treatment including crowns and bridges. Denplan Essentials, which for an average monthly fee of £12 covers just normal routine care including examinations, X-rays and hygienists' visits. In both cases, patients' actual monthly fees are calculated by their own dentist after an initial assessment of their oral health.

Among other benefits, membership of Denplan entitles you to emergency treatment of up to £740 per claim, accident insurance cover of up to £10,000 per claim and access to a 24-hour helpline. Registration must of course be with a Denplan member dentist but as around a third of UK dentists participate this should not be a problem. For further information, contact: **Denplan Ltd:** Tel: 01962 828000; e-mail: hr@denplan.co.uk; website: www.denplan.co.uk.

Prevention is always better than cure. If you want free, independent and impartial advice on all aspects of oral health and free literature on a wide range of topics, including patients' rights, finding a dentist and dental care for older people, contact: **The British Dental Health Foundation:** Tel: 0870 770 4000; e-mail: mail@dentalhealth.org; website: www.dentalhealth.org.uk.

Another useful free factsheet is *Dental Care* from Age Concern. Contact: Tel: 0800 00 99 66; website: www.ageconcern.org.uk.

Personal relationships

Retirement, for couples, is a bit like getting married again. It involves a new lifestyle, fresh opportunities and inevitably, as with marriage, a few compromises are needed. He will have to accustom himself to no longer going to a regular job. She will have to start thinking about another meal to prepare and may possibly feel compelled to reorganise her domestic or working routine. Alternatively, of course, it could be the other way round. If the wife has given up her job, the husband, if he has long acted as manager of the household, may be worrying at the prospect of someone carrying out spot checks on his activities at regular intervals.

After years of perhaps seeing each other no more than a couple of hours at the beginning and end of each weekday, suddenly almost the whole of every day can be spent together. He may feel hurt that she does not appear more delighted. She may feel guilty about wanting to pursue her normal activities. More and more women are nowadays working after the husband has retired. Sometimes too, with the children no longer at home, couples may feel they have nothing left in common. There is a sad statistic that indicates this may be true; there has been a recent increase in the over-60s divorce rate. It is possible therefore that one or other of the couple may be tempted to seek excitement elsewhere rather than trying to work out a solution together.

It is possible that even in the most loving relationship, the first weeks of retirement – for either partner – can produce tensions. This may consequently affect their sex life in a way that neither had anticipated. Normally with goodwill and understanding on both sides difficulties are quickly resolved to allow an even deeper, more satisfying relationship to develop. However, for some couples it does not work out so easily and it may be helpful to seek skilled guidance.

Relate offers a counselling service to people who are experiencing difficulties in their marriage or other personal relationships. Their clients are of all ages. Some have been married twice or even three times. Many are in the throes of actually seeking a divorce but are trying to prevent the bitterness that can develop. Some come for advice because of upsets with their stepchildren. Others may have sexual problems. Sometimes couples come together. Sometimes, either the husband or the wife comes alone. Often, the emphasis is not on a particular crisis but instead on ways couples are seeking to make their marriage more positively enjoyable, as at retirement.

Relate offers counselling through 88 centres around the country. Each counselling centre operates an independent pricing policy and counsellors will discuss with clients what they can reasonably contribute. However, no one is turned away if they cannot afford to make a contribution. Local branches can be found by contacting: **Relate England:** Tel: 0300 100 1234; website: www.relate.org.uk. **Relate Scotland:** Tel: 0845 119 6088; website: www.relatescotland. org.uk.

Marriage Care offers a similar service, plus a confidential telephone helpline, for those who are having problems with their marriage or other close personal relationship. **Marriage Care England and Wales:** Tel: 0845 660 6000; website: www.marriagecare.org.uk. **Scottish Marriage Care:** Tel: 0141 222 2166; website: www.scottishmarriagecare.org.

Another organisation that may be of interest is Albany Trust, which offers counselling for people facing change and with difficulties in relationships, depression or psychosexual problems. Costs vary, but fees are negotiable for those on low income. Contact: **Albany Trust**: Tel: 020 8767 1827; e-mail: info@albanytrust.org; website: www.albanytrust.org.

Help for grandparents

A sad result of today's divorce statistics is the risk to grand-parents of losing contact with their grandchildren. Although some divorcing parents lean over backwards to avoid this happening, others – maybe through force of circumstances or hurt feelings – deny grandparents access or even sever the relationship completely. Until 1989 grandparents had very few rights. However, following the introduction of the Children Act, grandparents may, with the leave of the court, seek an order for contact with the child or for residence so that the child may live with them. Generally, a fee is payable to the court for the making of such applications unless the grandparent is in receipt of community legal service funding (formerly legal aid). In reaching a decision the paramount consideration for the court must be what action, if any, is in the best interest of the child. If the court feels that the child is of sufficient age and under-standing, it will take into account his/her views in reaching a decision.

Recourse to the law is never a step to be taken lightly and should obviously be avoided if there is the possibility that a more conciliatory approach could be successful. An organisation that has considerable experience of advising grandparents and that can also offer a mediation service in London, as well as practical help and support with legal formalities, is **Grandparents' Association:** Tel: 0845 434 9585; e-mail: info@grandparents-association.org.uk; website: www.grandparents-association.org.uk.

Depression

Depression is a condition that is often akin to problems in a marriage and other personal crises. It is fairly common after giving birth, as well as after bereavement. It can be caused by worries or may occur after an operation. Sometimes too, as a number of retired people find, it develops as a result of loneliness, boredom or general lack of purpose. Usually, people manage to deal with it alone. They come out of it in their own way and in their own time, depending on how quickly time heals sorrow or the scars of a relationship that has gone wrong. In the case of those who are temporarily bored and fed up, they will recover as soon as they find new interests and outlets for their talents.

If the condition persists for more than a few days, a doctor should always be consulted, as depression can create sleeping difficulties. It also affects the appetite and leads to an overall feeling of physical malaise. The sufferer can be caught in a vicious circle of being too listless to enjoy anything, yet not having done enough during the day to be able to sleep at the proper time.

Another reason for consulting a doctor is that depression may be due to being physically run down. If you've recently suffered from flu, maybe all that is required is a good tonic – or perhaps a holiday. Sometimes, however, depression persists. In these cases it may be that rather than medicines or the stimulus of a new activity, individuals may feel the need to talk to someone. Often it is better to find someone outside the family circle who has a deeper understanding of what they are experiencing. There are several organisations that may be able to help.

Depression Alliance is a charity that offers assistance to anyone affected by depression. As well as a nationwide network of groups where individuals can meet to provide mutual support, Depression Alliance has a pen-friend scheme and also produces a quarterly newsletter and a wide range of free literature. For further information, contact: Tel: 0845 123 23 20; e-mail: information@depression alliance.org; website: www.depressionalliance.org.

Samaritans are available at any time of the day or night, every single day of the year. They are there to talk or listen for as long as an individual needs or wants to be able to speak to another person. Although most people think of Samaritans as being a telephone service for those who feel they may be in danger of taking their own lives, anyone who would like to can visit their local branch. You do not need to feel actively suicidal before contacting Samaritans; if you are simply depressed, they will equally welcome your call. The service is free and completely confidential, just contact: Tel: 08457 90 90 90; e-mail: jo@samaritans.org; website: www.samaritans.org.

Mind (National Association for Mental Health – NAMH) works for a better life for people with experience of mental distress. It has offices in England and Wales and more than 200 local associations that offer a wide range of special facilities and services, including housing with care, day centres, social clubs, advocacy and self-help groups. Mind also runs a national information line and produces a variety of publications including a bi-monthly magazine. For further information, contact: Tel: 0845 766 0163; e-mail: contact@mind.org.uk; website: www.mind.org.uk.

Sane is a mental health charity that, in addition to initiating and funding research, operates a helpline to give individuals in need of emotional support or practical information the help they require. It can provide information about local and national mental health services, mental health law and the rights of both service users and carers. SANELINE is open every day, from 1 pm to 11 pm. Contact: Tel: 0845 767 8000; e-mail: info@sane.org.uk; website: www.sane. org.uk.

Some common afflictions

Quite probably you will be one of the lucky ones and the rest of this chapter will be of no further interest to you. It deals with some of the more common afflictions, such as back pain and heart disease, as well as with disability. However, if you are unfortunate enough to be affected, or have a member of your family who is, then knowing which organisations can provide support could make all the difference in helping you to cope.

Aphasia

Aphasia is a condition that makes it hard to speak, read or understand language. It typically affects individuals after a stroke or a head injury. Speakability is the national charity offering information and support to people with aphasia, their families and carers. As well as a helpline, it has fact-sheets, publications and videos. There is also a national network of self-help groups. For further information, contact: **Speakability** (Action for Dysphasic Adults): Tel: 0808 808 9572; e-mail: speakability@speakability.org.uk; website: www.speakability.org.uk.

Arthritis and rheumatism

Although arthritis is often thought of as an older person's complaint, it accounts for the loss of an estimated 70 million working days a year in Britain. **Arthritis Care** is a registered charity working with, and for, people with arthritis. It encourages self-help and has over 400 local branches offering practical support and social activities. There is a confidential helpline, staffed by professional counsellors, open 10 am to 4 pm weekdays. Arthritis Care also runs four specially adapted hotels and publishes various leaflets and booklets. For the addresses of local branches, contact: Arthritis Care: Tel: 0808 600 6868; e-mail: info@arthritis-care.org.uk; website: www.arthritiscare.org.uk.

In addition to funding a major research programme, **Arthritis Research Campaign** (arc), publishes a large number of free booklets on understanding and coping with arthritis and also produces a quarterly magazine *Arthritis Today*.

Contact: Tel: 0870 850 5000; e-mail: info@arc.org.uk; website: www.arc.org.uk.

Back pain

Four out of five people suffer from back pain at some stage of their lives. Although there are many different causes, doctors agree that much of the trouble could be avoided through correct posture, care in lifting heavy articles, a firm mattress and chairs that provide support in the right places. Whether you have problems or are hoping to prevent them, the following two organisations could be helpful.

The Back Shop is a shop and mail-order business that sells ergonomically approved products that help prevent back trouble or may provide relief for those who suffer. The shop is staffed by assistants with specialised knowledge of back pain and related problems. Contact: Tel: 020 7935 9120; e-mail: info@thebackshop.co.uk; website: www.theback-shop.co.uk.

BackCare is a registered charity that funds research into the causes and treatment of back pain and also publishes a range of leaflets and factsheets to help back-pain sufferers. It has local branches around the country that organise talks, lectures and exercise classes as well as social activities and fundraising events. Membership includes copies of the quarterly magazine, *Talkback*. Contact: Tel: 0845 130 2704; e-mail: website@backcare.org.uk; website: www.backpain.org.uk.

Cancer

One of the really excellent trends in recent years is a far greater willingness to talk about cancer. Quite apart from the fact that discussing the subject openly has removed some of the dread, increasingly one hears stories of many more people who have made a complete recovery. Early diagnosis can make a vital difference. Doctors recommend that all women should undergo regular screening for cervical cancer and women over 50 are advised to have a routine mammography to screen for breast cancer at least once every three years.

Computerised cervical screening systems for women aged 25 to 64 and breast cancer screening units for women aged 50 to 70 are available nationwide. In both cases, older women can have access to the services on request. It also goes without saying that anyone with a lump or swelling, however small, should waste no time in having it investigated by a doctor. There are a number of excellent support groups for cancer sufferers. Rather than list them all, we have only included two, as Cancerbackup, as well as its own services, can act as an information service about other local cancer support groups.

Cancerbackup offers a free and confidential telephone information service to help people affected by cancer. Calls are answered by a qualified nurse who has the time, knowledge and understanding to answer your questions and listen to how you may be feeling. Cancerbackup also produces many booklets and factsheets on different types of cancer and their treatment. A publications list is available via their website. Contact: Tel: 0808 800 1234; website: www.cancerbackup. org.uk.

Breast Cancer Care offers practical advice, information and emotional support to women who have, or fear they have, breast cancer or benign breast disease. Its services include a helpline, free leaflets, a prosthesis-fitting service and one-to-one support from volunteers who have themselves experienced breast cancer or whose partner has been affected. Interactive support from both professionals and people affected by breast cancer is available via their website. Contact: Tel: 0808 800 6000; email: info@breastcancercare.org.uk; website: www.breastcancercare.org.uk.

Chest and heart diseases

The earlier sections on smoking, diet, drink and exercise list some of the most pertinent 'dos and don'ts' that can help prevent heart disease. The advice is not to be taken lightly. Latest statistics reveal that UK death rates from coronary heart disease are among the highest in the world, killing almost 120,000 people a year and responsible for one in five of all deaths. Although people tend to think of heart attacks as particularly affecting men, over four times as many women die from heart disease as from breast cancer. In an effort to reduce the casualty rate, the British Heart Foundation publishes a range of 'help yourself' booklets, designed to create greater awareness of how heart disease can best be prevented through healthy living. For further information, contact: **British Heart Foundation**: Tel: 0300 333 1333; website: www.bhf.org.uk.

Diabetes

Diabetes occurs when the amount of glucose in the blood is too high for the body to use properly. It can sometimes be treated by diet alone; sometimes pills or insulin may also be needed. Diabetes can be diagnosed at any age, though it is common in the elderly and especially among individuals who are overweight. Diabetes UK aims to improve the lives of people with diabetes. It offers information and support to affected individuals, their families and friends. There are around 430 nationwide branches that hold regular meetings and social activities. Contact **Diabetes UK**: Tel: 0845 120 2960; e-mail: info@diabetes.org.uk; website: www.diabetes.org.uk.

Migraine

Migraine affects over 10 million people in the United Kingdom. It can involve severe head pains, nausea, vomiting, visual disturbances and in some cases temporary paralysis. The Migraine Trust funds and promotes research, holds international symposia and runs an extensive support service. Contact: Tel: 020 7462 6601; e-mail: info@migraine trust.org; website: www.migrainetrust.org.

Osteoporosis and menopause problems

Osteoporosis is a disease affecting bones, in which they become so fragile that they can break very easily, with injuries most common in the spine, hip and wrist. It affects one in two women (also one in five men) and often develops following the menopause when body levels of oestrogen naturally decrease.

The **National Osteoporosis Society** offers help, support and advice on all aspects of osteoporosis. There is a medical helpline staffed by specialist nurses, a range of leaflets and booklets and also a network of over 120 local support groups throughout the United Kingdom. Contact: Tel: 0845 450 0230; e-mail: info@nos.org.uk; website: www.nos.org. uk.

Women's Health Concern (WHC) is a national charity, founded in 1972 to offer professional advice and counselling to women, in particular those with gynaecological and hormonal disturbance problems, as well as with the menopause. It runs a telephone and e-mail nurse counselling service. Factsheets and general information about gynaecological conditions can be sourced from the website. As a charity, WHC charges no fee but donations are very much appreciated. For further information, contact: Tel: 0845 123 2319; e-mail: info@womens-health-concern.org; website: www.womens-health-concern.org.

The Menopause Exchange produces a quarterly newsletter and number of factsheets with the aim of providing reliable and easily understood information about the menopause and other health issues of concern to women in midlife. There is also an information service and members have access to an 'Ask the Experts' panel. Contact: Tel: 020 8420 7245; e-mail: norma@menopause-exchange.co.uk.

Stroke

Over 130,000 people suffer a stroke every year in England and Wales. A stroke is a brain injury caused by the sudden interruption of blood flow. It is unpredictable in its effects, which may include muscular paralysis or weakness on one side, loss of speech or loss of understanding or language, visual problems or incontinence. Prevention is similar to the prevention of heart disease.

The Stroke Association works to prevent strokes and helps stroke patients and their families. It produces a range of publications and provides advice and welfare grants to individuals through its London office and regional centres. Its Community Services, Dysphasia Support and Family Support help stroke sufferers through home visits, and over 400 stroke clubs provide social and therapeutic support. Contact: Tel: 0845 303 3100; e-mail: info@stroke.org.uk; website: www.stroke.org.uk.

Some special problems

A minority of people, as they become older, suffer from special problems that can cause great distress. Because families do not like to talk about them, they may be unaware of what services are available, so may be missing out both on practical help and sometimes also on financial assistance.

Hypothermia

Elderly people tend to be more vulnerable to the cold. If the body drops below a certain temperature, it can be dangerous because one of the symptoms of hypothermia is that sufferers no longer actually feel cold. Instead, they may lose their appetite and vitality and may become mentally confused. Instead of doing all the sensible things like getting a hot drink and putting on an extra sweater, they are liable to neglect themselves further and can put themselves at real risk.

Although heating costs are often blamed, quite wealthy people can also be victims by allowing their home to become too cold or not wearing sufficient clothing. For this reason, during a cold snap it is very important to check up regularly on an elderly person living alone.

British Gas, electricity companies and the Solid Fuel Association are all willing to give advice on how heating systems can be used more efficiently and economically. (See telephone directory for nearest branch or ask at the Citizens Advice Bureau.) Insulation can also play a very large part in keeping a home warmer and cheaper to heat. It may be possible to obtain a grant from the local authority, although normally this would only be likely on grounds of real need.

Additionally, elderly and disabled people in receipt of income support may receive a cold weather payment to help with heating costs during a particularly cold spell: that is, when the temperature is forecast to drop to zero degrees Celsius (or below) for seven consecutive days. The amount paid is £8.50 a week. Those eligible should receive the money automatically. In the event of any problem, ask at your social security office. In the event of any emergency, such as a power cut, contact the Citizens Advice Bureau or local Age Concern group.

Finally, every household with someone aged 60 or older will get an annual tax-free winter fuel payment of £200, while those with a resident aged 80 or older will receive £400. For further information, telephone the **Winter Fuel Payment Helpline** on Tel: 08459 15 15 15; website: www.thepension service.gov.uk.

Incontinence

Bladder or bowel problems can cause deep embarrassment to sufferers as well as inconvenience to relatives. The problems can occur in an elderly person for all sorts of reasons and a doctor should always be consulted, as it can often be cured or at least alleviated by proper treatment. To assist with the practical problems, some local authorities operate a laundry service that collects soiled linen, sometimes several times a week. The person to talk to is the health visitor or district nurse (telephone your local health centre), who will be able to advise about this and other facilities.

Incontact (a new charity launched in September 2008, following the closure of the Continence Foundation in May 2008) is for people with bladder and bowel dysfunction. This charity incorporates and continues the work of the Continence Foundation and operates a helpline that is staffed by nurses with a special understanding of bladder and bowel problems. For further information, contact: Tel:

0870 770 3246; e-mail: info@incontact.org; website: www.incontact.org.

Useful reading

Product information and free booklets on continence care are available from Coloplast Ltd. For further details, contact: Tel: 01733 392000; website: www.coloplast.co.uk.

Dementia

Sometimes an elderly person can become confused or forgetful, suffer severe loss of memory or have violent mood swings and at times be abnormally aggressive. It is important to consult a doctor as soon as possible as the cause may be depression, stress or even vitamin deficiency. All of these can be treated and often completely cured. If dementia is diagnosed, there are ways of helping a sufferer to cope better with acute forgetfulness and other symptoms.

The most common type of dementia is Alzheimer's disease, which is usually found in people aged over 65. Approximately 24 million people worldwide have dementia, of which the majority (over 60 per cent) is due to Alzheimer's.

Clinical signs are characterised by progressive cognitive deterioration, together with a decline in the ability to carry out common daily tasks and behavioural changes. The first readily identifiable symptoms of Alzheimer's disease are usually short-term memory loss and visual-spatial confusion. These initial symptoms progress from seemingly simple and fluctuating to a more pervasive loss of memory, including difficulty navigating familiar areas such as the local neighbourhood. This advances to loss of other familiar and well-known skills as well as recognition of objects and persons.

Since family members are often the first to notice changes that might indicate the onset of Alzheimer's (or other forms of dementia) they should learn the early warning signs. They should serve as informants during initial evaluation of patients clinically. It is important to consult your doctor as soon as you have concerns. It is also a good idea to talk to the health visitor, as they will know about any helpful facilities that may be available locally. They are also able to arrange appointments with other professionals, such as the community psychiatric nurse and occupational therapist.

The charity **Mind** can often also help. Addresses to contact are:

Mind (National Association for Mental Health – NAMH): Tel: 020 8519 2122; e-mail: contact@mind.org.uk; website: www.mind.org.uk.

Mind Cymru: Tel: 029 2039 5123; website: www. mind.org.uk.

Scottish Association for Mental Health: Tel: 0141 568 7000; website: www.mind.org.uk.

Northern Ireland Association for Mental Health: Tel: 028 9032 8474; website: www.mind.org.uk.

There are two other helpful organisations giving support to people with dementia and their carers. The **Alzheimer's Society**; for further information, contact: Tel: 0845 300 0336; email: enquiries@alzheimers.org.uk; website: www.alzheimers.org.uk. **Alzheimer Scotland – Action on Dementia** has local services throughout Scotland; for addresses and other information, contact: Tel: 0808 808 3000; website: www.alzscot.org.

Useful reading

Caring for the Person with Dementia, published by the Alzheimer's Society, £7 including p&p. Website: www.alzheimers.org.uk.

Understanding Dementia, £1, available from Mind Mail Order Service. Website: www.mind.org.uk at the address listed above.

3

Disability

Disability is something many people have to face in life. If you or someone in your family has a problem, here is a list of some key organisations that can help you plus one or two other points that may be useful for younger people.

Local authority services

Social services departments (social work department in Scotland) provide many of the services that people with disabilities may need, including:

- practical help in the home, perhaps with the support of a home help;

░ adaptations to your home, such as a ramp for a wheel-chair or other special equipment for your safety;

░ meals on wheels;

░ provision of day centres, clubs and similar;

░ issue of badges for cars driven or used by people with a disability (in some authorities this is handled by the works department or by the residents' parking department);

░ advice about other transport services or concessions that may be available locally.

In most instances, you should speak to a social worker, who will either be able to make the arrangements or signpost you in the right direction. He/she will also be able to tell you of any special facilities or other help provided by the authority.

Occupational therapists, who can advise about special equipment and help teach someone with a disability how best to manage through training and exercise, also come within the orbit of the social services department.

Health care

Services are normally arranged through either a GP or the local authority health centre. Key professional staff include:

░ health visitors: qualified nurses who, rather like social workers, will be able to put you in touch with whatever specialised services are required;

district nurses: who will visit patients in their home;

physiotherapists: who use exercise and massage to help improve mobility, for example after an operation;

medical social workers (employed at hospitals): who will help with any arrangements before a patient is discharged.

Employment

The disablement resettlement officer helps and advises people looking for work and can also give information about any available grants, for example towards the cost of fares to work and for special equipment that may make work life easier. Ask at your nearest Jobcentre or Jobcentre Plus office: website: www.jobcentreplus.gov.uk.

Council tax

If someone in your family has a disability, you may be able to claim a reduction on your council tax. If you have an orange badge on your car, you may get a rebate for a garage. You would normally apply to the housing benefits officer but different councils employ different officers to deal with this. Website: www.dwp.gov.uk.

Equipment

If you have temporary need of, say, a wheelchair, you will normally be able to borrow this from the hospital or your local British Red Cross branch. If you want equipment including aids for the home on a more permanent basis, one of the best sources of information is the Disabled Living Foundation Equipment Centre, where all sorts of equipment can be seen and tried out by visitors. Information advisers are on hand to demonstrate the equipment and to give advice. For more details, contact: **Disabled Living Foundation**: Tel: 0845 130 9177; e-mail: advice@dlf.org.uk; website: www.dlf.org.uk.

Assist UK will recommend a centre nearer your home, should you be unable to travel. Contact: Tel: 0870 770 2866; e-mail: general.info@assist-uk.org; website: www. assist-uk.org.

Finally, **BT** publishes a useful guide entitled *Communications Solutions* with information for those who have difficulty in using a standard telephone. For further information and a free copy, call: Tel: 0800 800 150; website: www.bt. com.

Other helpful organisations

Royal Association for Disability and Rehabilitation (RADAR) helps with the National Key Scheme for Toilets for Disabled People. About 400 local authorities throughout the country have fitted standard locks to their loos – and issue keys to disabled people – so that the facilities can be used by them, even when these would normally be locked against vandalism. RADAR supplies keys at a charge of £3.50 incl p&p for those who are unable to obtain an NKS key in their own locality. Applicants must state their name and address together with a declaration of disability. For further information, contact: Tel: 020 7250 3222; email: radar@radar.org.uk; website: www.radar.org.uk.

Age Concern England runs the Ageing Well UK Programme. Over 160 local projects recruit volunteer 'senior health mentors' to encourage people of their own generation to improve and maintain their health. For further information, contact ActivAge Unit: Tel: 020 8765 7231; e-mail: aau@ace.org.uk; website: www.ageconcern.org.uk.

Disability Alliance publishes a number of free factsheets and also an annual *Disability Rights Handbook*, which is packed with information about benefits and services both for people with disabilities and for their families. Contact: Tel: 020 7247 8776; e-mail: office.da@dial.pipex.com; website: www.disabilityalliance.org.

Disability Wales/Anabledd Cymru strives to achieve rights, equality and choice for all disabled people in Wales. Tel: 029 2088 7325; e-mail: info@disabilitywales.org; website: www.disabilitywales.org.

Help the Hospices is a national charity dedicated to the support of hospices, their special day centres and home care teams, and other providers of palliative care for terminally ill people and their families. For a list of independent charitable hospices, which are free to patients, and other information, contact: Tel: 020 7520 8200; e-mail: info@helpthehospices.org.uk; website: www.helpthehospices.org.uk.

Wellbeing. A free health information service, essentially for people in Scotland. Contact: Tel: 0141 248 1899; email: well@scotland.gsi.gov.uk; website: www.wellscotland.info.

Transport

The difficulty of getting around is often a major problem for elderly and disabled people. In addition to the facilities run by voluntary organisations already mentioned, there are several other very useful services.

London Taxicard Scheme. A scheme whereby disabled people can use a taxi weekdays and weekends at a much reduced rate, subsidised by their local authority. Prices may vary depending on in which borough the person is resident. The fleet includes taxis capable of accommodating wheelchairs. A leaflet and application form are obtainable from local authority social services departments or The Association of London Government (Taxicard). Contact: Tel: 020 7484 2929; e-mail: taxicard@londoncouncils.gov.uk; website: www.taxicard.org.uk.

The Forum of Mobility Centres provides information on a network of independent organisations throughout England, Scotland, Wales and Northern Ireland to help individuals who have a medical condition or are recovering from an accident or injury that may affect their ability to drive. For details of your nearest centre, contact: Tel: 0800 559 3636; email: mobility@rcht.cornwall.nhs.uk; website: www.mobility-centres.org.uk.

Motability is a registered charity set up to assist recipients of the War Pensioners' Mobility Supplement and/or the higher-rate mobility component of disability living allowance to use their allowance to lease, or buy, a car or a powered wheel-chair or scooter. Motability's charitable fund can help those unable to afford the advance payment on some lease vehicles – or necessary adaptations to the vehicle. Grants are available for the least expensive option to meet individuals' basic mobility needs. Contact: Tel: 0845 456 4566; website: www.motability.co.uk.

Driving licence renewal at age 70

All drivers aged 70 are sent a licence renewal form to have their driving licence renewed. The licence has to be renewed at least every three years. Depending on the individual's health, including in particular their eyesight, the driver might be sent a new form to complete after only one or two years. If you have any queries or if three weeks after returning the form, your new licence has not arrived, contact the **DVLA** Customer Enquiries: Tel: 0870 240 0009; website: www.dvla.gov.uk.

Powers of attorney

Around the late-60s, many perfectly fit men and women wonder whether it might be sensible to give power of attorney to someone they trust. This involves authorising another person to take business and other financial decisions on their behalf, on the basis that any such decisions would reflect the action that they themselves would have taken. Until a few years ago, the power could only be used where the individual was unwilling rather than incapable of acting for him/herself. So in effect, just at the time when the power was most needed, it ceased to exist.

Thanks to a law known as the Enduring Powers of Attorney Act 1985, and the more recent Lasting Powers of Attorney (see below) an enduring power is not automatically revoked by any subsequent mental incapacity, but can now continue, regardless of any decline, throughout the individual's life. (**NB:** An ordinary power of attorney would be revoked by subsequent mental incapacity.) To protect the donor and the nominated attorney, the Act clearly lays down certain principles that must be observed, with both sides signing a declaration that they understand the various rights and duties involved. The Act furthermore calls for the power to be formally registered with the Public Trust Office in the event of the donor being, or becoming, mentally incapable.

As stated above, the Enduring Powers of Attorney have been replaced by Lasting Powers of Attorney (LPA), to coincide with the implementation of the Mental Capacity Act 2005. In effect, LPAs enable individuals to give their attorney power to make decisions about their personal welfare, including health care, when they lack the capacity to make such decisions themselves. Enduring Powers of Attorney, set up before October 2007, are still effective. However, if you have not yet set one up but are planning to do so, you will now need to apply for the new LPA instead.

As any lawyer would explain, the right time to give power of attorney is when the individual is in full command of his/her faculties, so that potential situations that would require decisions can be properly discussed and the donor's wishes made clear. For the Lasting Power of Attorney to be valid, the donor must in any event be capable of understanding what he/she is agreeing to at the time of making the power.

There are two ways of drawing up a Lasting Power of Attorney: either through a solicitor or by buying a standard form published by Oyez, available by phone from **OyezStraker Group Ltd** on Tel: 0870 737 7370. It is sensible for people without a legal background to consult a solicitor. For further information contact **The Office of the Public Guardian**: Tel: 0845 330 2900; e-mail: customerservices@ publicguardian.gsi.gov.uk; website: www.publicguardian. gov.uk.

Temporary living-in help

Elderly people living alone can be more vulnerable to flu and other winter ailments. They may have a fall; or, for no apparent reason, may go through a period of being forgetful and neglecting themselves. Equally, as they become older, they may not be able to cope as well with managing their home or caring for themselves. In the event of an emergency or if you have reason for concern – perhaps because you are going on holiday and will not be around to keep a watchful eye – engaging living-in help can be a godsend. Most agencies tend inevitably to be on the expensive side, although in the event of a real problem they often represent excellent value for money. A more unusual and interesting longer-term possibility is to recruit the help of a Community Service Volunteer.

Community Service Volunteers (CSVs) who are aged over 16, are involved in a variety of projects nationwide. CSV's Independent Living Projects match full-time helpers with individuals and families who need a high degree of support. The volunteers are untrained and work for periods of 4 to 12 months away from home. They take their instructions from the people for whom they are working, but are not of course substitutes for professional carers. In general they provide practical assistance in the home including, for example, shopping, light cooking, tidying up, attending to the garden and sometimes also decorating jobs. They also offer companionship.

Usually a care scheme is set up through a social worker, who supervises how the arrangement is working out. Volunteers are placed on a one month's trial basis. Contact your local social services department; or approach CSV direct for further information. Tel: 020 7278 6601; e-mail: information@csv.org.uk; website: www.csv.org.uk.

Agencies

The agencies listed specialise in providing temporary help, rather than permanent staff. Charges vary, but in addition to the weekly payment to helpers, there is normally an agency booking fee. As a rule payment is gross, so you will not be involved in having to work out tax or National Insurance.

Consultus Care & Nursing Agency Ltd. Tel: 01732 355231; e-mail: office@consultuscare.com; website: www.consultus-care.com.

Country Cousins. Tel: 0845 601 4003; website: www. country-cousins.co.uk.

Universal Aunts Ltd. Tel: 020 7738 8937; e-mail: aunts@ universalaunts.co.uk; website: www.universalaunts. co.uk.

For a further list of agencies, see *The Lady* magazine, or search the internet under heading 'Employment' or 'Care' agencies or look at website www.yell.com for addresses in your local area.

Nursing care

If someone in your family needs regular nursing care, their doctor may be able to arrange for a community or district nurse to visit them at home. This will not, of course, be a sleeping-in arrangement but simply involves a qualified nurse calling round when necessary. If you want more concentrated home nursing you will have to go through a private agency. Consultus can sometimes supply trained nurses. Additionally, there are many specialist agencies that can arrange hourly, daily or living-in nurses on a temporary or longer-term basis.

Terms of employment vary considerably. Some nurses will literally undertake nursing duties only – and nothing else; and may even expect to have their meals provided. Others will do light housework and act as nurse-companions. Fees vary throughout the country, with London inevitably being most expensive. Private health insurance can sometimes be claimed against part of the cost, but this is generally only in respect of qualified nurses.

Your local health centre or social services department should be able to give you names and addresses of local agencies. Alternatively, search the internet under heading 'Nursing Agencies' or look at website www.yell.com for addresses in your local area.

Permanent living-in help

There may come a time when you feel that it is no longer safe to live entirely on your own. One possibility is to engage a companion or housekeeper on a permanent basis but such arrangements are normally very expensive: the going rate for housekeepers in London is anything between £400 and £700 a week clear. However, if you want to investigate the idea further, many domestic agencies (see the *Yellow Pages* or the website www.yell.com) supply housekeeper-companions. Alternatively, you might consider advertising in *The Lady*, which is probably the most widely read publication for these kinds of post. For further details: *The Lady* **magazine**: Tel: 020 7379 4717; e-mail: editors@lady.co.uk; website: www.lady.co.uk.

Permanent help can also sometimes be provided by agencies (such as those listed under 'Temporary living-in help'), who will supply continuous four-weekly placements. This is an expensive option and the lack of continuity can at times be distressing for elderly people, particularly at the change-over point. But it can also lead to a happier atmosphere as the housekeeper comes fresh to the job and neither party has time to start getting on each other's nerves. See:

Consultus Care & Nursing Agency Ltd. Tel: 01732 355231; email: office@consultuscare.com; website: www.consultus-care.com.

Country Cousins. Tel: 0845 601 4003; website: www. country-cousins.co.uk.

Universal Aunts Ltd. Tel: 020 7738 8937; e-mail: aunts@ universalaunts.co.uk; website: www.universalaunts. co.uk.

Au pairs are cheaper: roughly £55 to £70 a week with full board and lodging. A drawback, however, is that most au pairs speak inadequate English (at least when they first arrive), and as they are technically students living 'en famille', they must by law be given plenty of free time to attend school and study. An alternative solution for some families is to engage a reliable daily woman who, in the event of illness or other problem, would be prepared to stay overnight.

Flexible care arrangements

One of the problems for many elderly people is that the amount of care they need is liable to vary according to the state of their health. There are other relevant factors including, for example, the availability of neighbours and family. Whereas after an operation the requirement may be for someone with basic nursing skills, a few weeks later the only need may be for someone to act as a companion. Under normal circumstances it may be as little as simply popping in for the odd hour during the day to cook a hot meal and check all is well. Few agencies cater for all the complex permutations that may be necessary in caring for an elderly person in their own home, but here are three that offer a genuinely flexible service:

Anchor Care workers can be engaged by the hour, or nightly, for temporary or longer periods, or on a more permanent residential basis. All staff are personally interviewed; their references are taken up and training is given. Prices vary according to the area and duties required. For further information contact: Tel: 020 8652 6566; website: www. anchor.org.uk.

Cura Domi – Care at Home carers undertake all or any of the tasks traditionally managed by a reliable housekeeper-companion. These include shopping, cooking, attending to the chores around the home, helping an elderly person bath or dress, reading aloud and generally providing whatever assistance may be needed. Where appropriate, carers can also provide all personal care and help needed with such problems as incontinence and dementia. Depending on what is required, they will come in for the hour or live in full time for a few days, a few weeks or longer. Great care is taken to try to match clients with a carer who possesses the right skills and temperament. All carers are backed by a team of RGN care managers on 24-hour call, seven days a week.

There is a once-only non-returnable registration/assessment fee with a list of varying prices according to whether the job is weekday, weekend, day-time, night-time or live-in. For further information contact: Tel: 01483 420055; website: www.curadomi.co.uk.

United Kingdom Home Care Association (UKHCA) represents over 1,500 member branches throughout the country that specialise in providing care for elderly and/or disabled people in their own home. All requirements are catered for including temporary and permanent posts, residential, daily, overnight and hourly work. UKHCA runs a Helpline – and also includes a 'Choosing care' section on its website – which can refer enquirers to local members committed to upholding the Association's Code of Practice. For further information contact: Tel: 020 8288 5291; e-mail: helpline@ukhca.co.uk; website: www.ukhca.co.uk.

Although any of these suggestions can work extremely well, many families find them either too expensive or haphazard – or both. So, sooner or later the decision may come down to a choice between residential care or moving in with relatives. Most families, to their credit, choose to care for an elderly parent in their own home. Sometimes, particularly in the case of a an unmarried son or daughter or other relative, it is more practical to move into their parents' (or relative's) home if the accommodation is more suitable.

Emergency care for pets

For many elderly people their pet is a most important part of their life; it provides companionship and fun as well as stimulating them into taking regular outdoor exercise. But in the event of the owner having to go into hospital or owing to some other emergency being temporarily unable to care for their pet, there can be real problems. These include not only concern for the welfare of the animal but often also considerable distress to the owner. To overcome these problems, two highly imaginative schemes have been set up. One operates throughout the United Kingdom and the other just in Scotland. Depending on what is required, volunteers will either simply feed or exercise the animal or will care for it in their own home until the owner can manage again.

Cinnamon Trust. As well as the above services, Cinnamon also offers permanent care for pets whose owners have died and who had registered their pets with the Trust. Some animals stay at the Trust's havens in Cornwall and Devon. Others are found alternative loving homes with a new owner. Either way, every effort is made to help pets adjust. Familiar possessions, such as the animal's basket or favourite toy, are very much encouraged and as far as possible 'families' of pets are kept together to avoid the further distress of separating them from their companions. Emergency services can be called 24-hours a day. The Trust makes no charge but donations, or a bequest, are very much appreciated. For further information contact: Tel: 01736 757900; e-mail: admin@cinnamon.org.uk; website: www. cinnamon.org.uk.

Pet Fostering Service Scotland. Here the focus is on temporary care. The only charges are the cost of a pet's food, litter – in the case of cats – and any veterinary fees that may be incurred during fostering. In the main the service caters for dogs, cats and birds, but some volunteers are willing to care for more exotic species such as rodents. If help is needed, contact: Tel: 01877 331 496; e-mail: info@pfss.org.uk; website: www.pfss.org.uk.

Practical help for carers

Although disability makes life more difficult, if you (or your family member) are still fairly active – visit friends, do your own shopping, enjoy some hobby that gets you out and about – the strains and difficulties may be fairly minimal. This applies particularly if your home lends itself to creating a self-contained annex, so everyone can retain some privacy and each person can continue to enjoy maximum independence. However, this is not always possible, and in the case of an ill or very frail person far more intensive care may be required. If you have to go out to work, need time to attend to other responsibilities or quite understandably feel that if you are to remain human you must have time for your own interests, it is important to know what help is available and how to obtain it.

The many services provided by local authorities and voluntary agencies, described earlier in the chapter, apply as much to an elderly person living with a family as to one living alone. If there is nothing in the list that solves a particular problem you may have, there are other courses of action. It would be sensible to talk to the Citizens Advice Bureau and social services department, as there may be some special local facility that could provide the solution.

It could also be useful to contact **The Princess Royal Trust for Carers**, which provides support services for carers throughout the United Kingdom and is a fund of practical information and advice. In particular, you might ask about **day centres and clubs**. Activities and surroundings vary, so you might wish to investigate. However, a responsible person will always be in charge and transport to and from the venue is often provided. For further information, contact: Tel: 0844 800 4361; e-mail: info@carers.org; website: www.carers.org.

You could also ask the local Age Concern group and WRVS. Age Concern will be able to tell you about the possibility of **voluntary sitters**: people who come in and stay with an elderly person for a few hours (or sometimes overnight), to prevent them from being on their own. **Age Concern:** website: www.ageconcern.org.uk; **WRVS** website: www. wrvs.org.uk. Other sources to try include the local branch of the **British Red Cross**: website: www.redcross.org; and the **St John Ambulance:** website: www.sja.org.uk.

Most areas now have, or are planning, **respite care facilities** to enable carers to take a break from their dependants from time to time. Depending on the circumstances, this could be for just the odd day or possibly for a week or two to enable carers who need it to have a real rest. A particularly welcome aspect of respite care is that many schemes specially cater for, among others, elderly people with dementia. For further information, contact your local health centre or social services department.

Another service well worth knowing about is **Crossroads**, which arranges for helpers to care for very frail or disabled people in their own home, while the regular carer is away. They will come in during the day, or stay overnight, and provide whatever practical help is required. Arrangements are planned very much on an individual basis and are tailored to meet particular family circumstances. Demand for the service is very high, so priority is given according to the strain imposed on the carer.

Both the Citizens Advice Bureau and social services department should be able to give you the address of the local branch. Alternatively, you could contact them directly: **Crossroads – Caring for Carers:** Tel: 0845 450 0350; website: www.crossroads.org.uk.

Holiday breaks for carers

There are various schemes to enable families with an elderly or disabled relative to go on holiday alone or simply to enjoy a respite from their caring responsibilities.

A number of local authorities run **fostering schemes**, on similar lines to child fostering. Elderly people are invited to stay in a neighbour's home and live in the household as an ordinary family member. Lasting relationships often develop. There may be a charge or the service may be run on a voluntary basis (or be paid for by the local authority). Schemes are patchy around the country. The Citizens Advice Bureau and social services department will advise you if anything exists.

Some voluntary organisations, including Age Concern groups and sometimes the Mothers' Union, organise **holidays for older people** to give relatives a break. Different charities take responsibility according to the area where you live: the Citizens Advice Bureau, volunteer centre or the social services department should know who you should approach. As with most types of provision, priority is given to families in greatest need.

You might also usefully contact **Tourism for All**, formerly known as Holiday Care, which, as well as advising on holidays for elderly and disabled people, can also advise carers who need a holiday about suitable provision for their dependent relative while they are away. For further information, contact: Tel: 0845 124 9971; e-mail: info@tourismforall.org.uk; website: www.tourismforall.org.uk.

Another solution is a **short-stay home**, which is residential accommodation variously run by local authorities, voluntary organisations or by private individuals, catering specifically for elderly people. Style and facilities vary from the very luxurious to the rather decrepit. For information about local authority provision, ask the social services department.

If, as opposed to general care, proper medical attention is necessary, you should consult your GP. Many **hospitals and nursing homes** offer short-stay care arrangements as a means of relieving relatives; a doctor should be able to help organise this for you.

The best place to seek a solution on anything to do with caring is:

Carers UK, which was set up to support and campaign for those caring for an ill, frail or disabled relative at home. There are around 80 self-help branches that are run for and by carers. Annual membership is from £10 and all members receive the magazine *Caring*. There is also a useful and informative website about all aspects of caring. For further information, contact: Tel: 0808 808 7777; e-mail: info@carersuk. org; website: www.carersuk.org.

Jewish Care runs a number of carers' groups, mostly in London. Contact Jewish Care head office for further information: Tel: 020 8922 2222; e-mail: jcdirect@jcare.org; website: www.jewishcare.org.

Useful reading

Caring for Someone? (SD4), available free from social security or Jobcentre Plus. Website: www.jobcentreplus.gov.uk.

Benefits and allowances

There are a number of benefits/allowances available to those with responsibility for the care of an elderly person and/or to elderly people themselves.

Entitlements for carers

Home responsibilities protection is a means of protecting your State pension if you are unable to work because of the necessity to care for an elderly person. For further details, ask for leaflet CF411 at any pension centre.

Carer's allowance. This used to be known as invalid care allowance but the name has been changed to highlight the fact that the allowance is paid as a benefit to carers. Men and women who spend at least 35 hours a week looking after a severely disabled person (ie someone who gets attendance allowance, constant attendance allowance or the two higher care components of disability living allowance) may qualify for carer's allowance. You do not need to be related to the person, nor do you need to live at the same address. Claimants may earn up to £95 a week after deduction of allowable expenses without loss of benefit.

For further details, enquire at your local Jobcentre Plus office or ring the Benefit Enquiry Line on: Tel: 0800 88 22 00; website: www.jobcentreplus.gov.uk.

Entitlements for elderly/disabled people

Higher personal allowance. People over 65 receive a higher personal allowance – £9,030 for those aged 65–74 and £9,180 for those aged 75 and over. The full amount is only given to people whose income does not exceed £21,800. People with higher incomes will have the age-related element of their personal allowance reduced by £1 for every £2 of income above the income limit. For further information, see IR leaflet 121 *Income Tax and Pensioners*. Website: www.hmrc.gov.uk.

Higher married couple's allowance. A higher married couple's allowance is similarly available to those couples where the elder partner is over 75. The current amount is £6,625, compared to the normal minimum of £2,540. Less-well-off couples aged between 65 (before 6 April 2000) and 74 receive £6,535. However, as with higher-rate personal allowance (see above), the full amount is only given to those whose income does not exceed £21,800.

Attendance allowance. This is paid to people aged 65 or over who are severely disabled, either mentally or physically, and have needed almost constant care for at least six months. (They may be able to get the allowance even if no one has actually given them that help.) An exception to the six months' qualifying period is made in the case of those who are terminally ill, who can receive the allowance without having to wait.

There are two rates of allowance: £67.00 a week for those needing 24-hour care, and £44.85 for those needing intensive day or night-time care. The allowance is tax-free and is generally paid regardless of income (although payment might be affected by entering residential care). For further details, together with a claim form, obtain leaflet DS 702 from social security offices and advice centres, or ring the Benefit Enquiry Line on: Tel: 0800 88 22 00; website: www.directgov.uk.

Disability living allowance (DLA). This benefit is paid to people who become disabled under the age of 65. It has two components: a mobility component and a care component. A person can be entitled either to one or to both components. The level of benefit depends on the person's care and/or mobility needs. There are two rates for the mobility component and three rates for the care component. The higher-rate mobility component, for people who are unable or virtually unable to walk, is £46.75 a week; the lower rate, for those who due to physical or mental disability need guidance or supervision in getting around, is £17.75. The three rates for the care component are: higher rate, £67.00; middle rate, £44.85; lower rate, £17.75. Disability living allowance is tax-free and is generally paid regardless of income (although payment might be affected by entering residential care). Except in the case of people who are terminally ill, who can receive the higher-rate care component of DLA immediately, there is a normal qualifying period of three months.

For further information, see leaflet DS 704 obtainable from Post Offices, Citizens Advice Bureaux and social security offices. The leaflet contains a reply slip, which you should complete and return as soon as possible in order to obtain the necessary claim pack. The pack includes a questionnaire with space for you to explain how the disability is making your life more difficult.

Cold weather payments. These are designed to give particularly vulnerable people extra help with heating costs during very cold weather. Anyone aged 60 and over who is in receipt of the guaranteed element of pension credit (formerly known as minimum income guarantee), income support or income-based jobseeker's allowance qualifies automatically. The payment is made by post as soon as the temperature in an area is forecast to drop – or actually drops – to zero degrees Celsius (or below) for seven consecutive days, so people can turn up their heating secure in the knowledge that they will be receiving extra cash help. The amount paid is £8.50 a week and those eligible should receive it without having to claim. In the event of a problem, contact your local Jobcentre Plus or social security office: website: www.jobcentreplus.gov.uk.

Winter fuel payments. This is a special annual tax-free payment of £200 given to all households with a resident aged 60 or older. Households with a resident aged 80 or older receive £400. Until fairly recently the payment only applied to households where someone had reached actual pension age. However, because the law has now been changed, men who missed out as a result of being under 65 may be able to claim a back payment for up to three years. To be able to claim for the full three years they would need to have been born by at latest 11 January 1938. The payments have been altered several times, so claims could only be for the amount that was payable at the time. Men who were aged 60 or more in 1997 when the payments first started and who think they might have a claim should ring the Helpline on: Tel: 08459 15 15 15 for further information. A number of women aged 60 or older may also have missed out on receiving the payment, most usually because they were not in receipt of a State pension. They too are advised to call the helpline above. Website: www.direct.gov.uk.

Free off-peak bus travel. Since 2008 people over the age of 60 and also disabled people can travel free on any bus service in the country.

Free TV licence. People aged 75 and older no longer have to pay for their TV licence.

Financial assistance

A number of charities give financial assistance to elderly people in need, including the following.

Counsel & Care gives advice on ways to fund care, whether this be for nursing/other residential care or for care in the home. Single needs payments are sometimes available to help towards holidays, special equipment, telephone installations and other priority items. For further information, contact: Tel: 0845 300 7585; e-mail: advice@counseland-care.org.uk; website: www.counselandcare.org.uk.

Elizabeth Finn Care gives grants to enable British and Irish people to remain in their own home and can also provide weekly grants to top up private care homes fees. For further information, contact: Tel: 020 7396 6700; e-mail: info@eliz-abethfinn.org.uk; website: www.elizabethfinntrust.org.uk.

Guild of Aid for Gentle People can assist those 'of gentle birth or good education' who want to stay in their own home and who cannot call on any professional/trade body. The Guild will also consider long-term help with fees in care homes. For further information, contact: Tel: 020 7935 0641; e-mail: thead@pcac.org.uk.

Independent Living Fund is a trust fund set up with government backing to assist people – aged 16 to 65 – with severe disabilities to pay for domestic or personal care to enable them to remain in their own home. To become eligible, applicants must first approach their local authority for assistance under the community care scheme and be successful in obtaining care services to the value of about

£200 a week. The Trust may top this up by up to an extra £455, provided: 1) they are living on their own or with someone who is unable to provide all the care they need; 2) they are receiving income support (or have a similar level of income once care has been paid); 3) they have savings of under £18,500; and 4) they receive the highest-rate care component of disability living allowance. For further information, contact: Tel: 0845 601 8815; e-mail: funds@ilf.org.uk; website: www.ilf.org.uk.

Independent Age helps older people to remain independent by providing small lifetime annuities, financial help in times of crisis and equipment to aid mobility. It also provides residential and nursing care and assistance with fees. For further information and free advice guide, entitled *60-Wise*, contact: Tel: 020 7605 4200; e-mail: charity@independentage.org.uk; website: www.independentage.org.uk.

Royal Agricultural Benevolent Institution (RABI) supports retired disabled or disadvantaged members of the farming community and their families, in England, Wales and Northern Ireland. Assistance includes a range of grants, help towards fees in residential and nursing homes and advice on other available support. RABI has two residential care homes and also sheltered flats available at Bury St Edmunds and Burnham-on-Sea, and nomination rights to other homes across England and Wales. For further information, contact: Tel: 01865 724931; e-mail: info@rabi.org.uk; website: www.rabi.org.uk.

SSAFA Forces Help is restricted to those who have served in the armed forces (including reservists and National Servicemen) and their families. Grants can be made to meet immediate need, including rent, wheelchairs and similar essentials. Contact via the local branch is preferred. For further details, contact: Tel: 0845 130 0975; e-mail: info@ ssafa.org.uk; website: www.ssafa.org.uk.

Wireless for the Bedridden Society loans radios and televisions on a permanent basis to elderly housebound people who cannot afford sets. Application should be made through a health visitor, social worker or officer of a recognised organisation. In the event of any queries re the procedure, contact: Tel: 01708 621101; e-mail: info@w4b.org.uk; website: www.w4b.org.uk.

Useful reading

For other sources of financial help, you could look at a copy of *A Guide to Grants for Individuals in Need*, published by the Directory of Social Change. Tel: 08450 77 77 07; e-mail: publications@dsc.org.uk; website: www.dsc.org.uk.

Helpful guidance

For many people one of the main barriers to getting help is knowing which of the many thousands of charities to approach.

Charity Search exists to help elderly people in need overcome their problem by putting them in contact with those charities most likely to be able to assist. For further information, contact the Secretary: Tel: 0117 982 4060; e-mail: info@charitysearch.org.uk; website: www.charitysearch. org.uk.

Summary

The information here is aimed to provide up-to-date and appropriate advice whether you are currently in the peak of condition or are beginning to feel the onset of age. There is much common-sense advice on how to keep fit and well, and who can give what help and how. The aim is for you to remain healthy and independent for as long as possible so that your retirement is enjoyable and trouble free. The list of organisations will be immensely useful should circumstances change and you need access to professional advice or sources of help. Prevention is always better than cure, so armed with the foregoing list of resources you will be provided with contact details of health care professionals and suitable organisations should you ever need them.

Notes

ALSO AVAILABLE FROM KOGAN PAGE

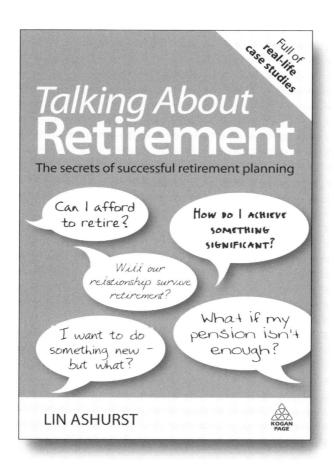

ISBN: 978 0 7494 5515 6   Paperback   2009

Order online now at www.koganpage.com

Sign up for regular e-mail updates on new
Kogan Page books in your interest area

The sharpest minds
need the finest advice

visit
www.koganpage.com
today

ALSO AVAILABLE FROM KOGAN PAGE

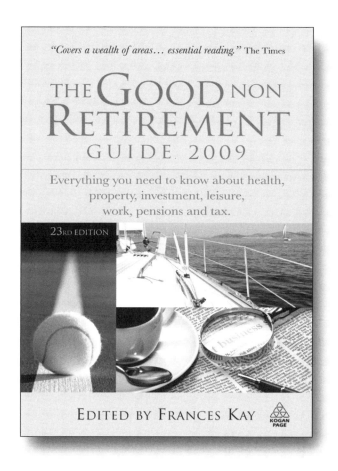

ISBN: 978 0 7494 5272 8   Paperback   2009